Praise for *Quiet Champions*

"Ian Chisholm's insights are a road map for anyone who wants to build a culture where people grow, learn and lead with purpose. Essential reading for leaders, coaches and those committed to making others better."
DANIEL COYLE, *New York Times*-bestselling author, *The Culture Code* and *The Talent Code*

"*Quiet Champions* is a powerful and inspiring celebration of the leadership our world truly needs—anchored in integrity, humility and an unwavering pursuit of excellence. Ian Chisholm doesn't just speak about leadership; he embodies it. His approach serves to uplift, nurtures authenticity and shapes stories that ignite real, lasting and meaningful change. This book is a must-read for anyone dedicated to cultivating leadership that creates deep and enduring impact across communities and organizations. *Quiet Champions* is not just a book—it's an energizing call to elevate the human spirit and lead with clarity, courage and purpose."
CAROL ANNE HILTON, CEO and founder, Indigenomics Institute, Global Centre of Indigenomics

"As someone who's spent a lifetime building businesses, I know first-hand that success is never a solo journey. In *Quiet Champions*, Ian Chisholm captures the heart of what truly matters in moving forward as a society: character, mentorship and passing the torch to our next generation of leaders. This book is a testament to the quiet, steady influence of mentors—those who guide, challenge and support us when the stakes are high. Every leader will find wisdom in these pages. Highly recommended."
JIM TRELIVING, Canadian entrepreneur and TV personality

"Ian Chisholm's *Quiet Champions* is your wake-up call: mentorship isn't about titles or noise, it's about the guts to show up and lift others—methodically, consistently and with a little quiet panache. If you're ready to be the mentor people actually want, this is your new playbook."
KYLA DUFRESNE, founder and CEO, Foxy Box

"Thoughtful. Honest. And important."
W. TIMOTHY GALLWEY, New York Times-bestselling author, The Inner Game of Tennis

"These ideas have shaped my journey of becoming a more authentic leader. Ian Chisholm has helped me to understand that the practice of leadership can happen anywhere and within anyone. *Quiet Champions* is a masterclass in how to find the key to unlock your greatest potential."
RYAN POMEROY, CEO, Pomeroy Lodging

"Ian Chisholm's philosophy has been the cornerstone of our corporate culture for the last twenty years. The Roy Group team continues to work with us to position our leaders as mentors in their communities and to our Fountain Tire teams across the country. We are excited that it is time for the wider world to be introduced to this approach."
JASON HERLE, CEO, Fountain Tire

"Ian Chisholm's insights remind us that the world's most impactful leaders are often those whose names aren't in the headlines, but whose influence echoes in every victory. If you want to understand how legacies are built and teams are transformed, this book is for you."
VICTOR CUI, co-founder, ONE Championship

"When addressing an audience of leaders, I once said: No client will remember you years from now, but every person who ever worked for you will remember everything you taught them about life and leadership. They'll remember who you were and how you infused them with that 'thing,' good or bad. This treatise gives life to that concept and helps you see how meaningful your life as a leader can be."
DAVID C. BAKER, "The Expert's Expert" (New York Times)

"These convictions about mentorship were the essential foundation of a powerful approach which I had the privilege of bringing to South Africa. This approach has not only unlocked human potential and agency in young leaders, but these leaders now form part of a national movement driving transformation of school culture and positive social change. Whenever I talk about the giants on whose shoulders we stood, I never fail to mention Ian Chisholm."
ROB TAYLOR, founder, Columba Leadership (South Africa)

QUIET CHAMPIONS

IAN CHISHOLM

QUIET CHAMPIONS

A WAY FORWARD *for* MENTORS
in TURBULENT TIMES

Copyright © 2025 by Ian Chisholm

All rights reserved. No part of this book may be reproduced, stored in a retrieval system or transmitted, in any form or by any means, without the prior written consent of the publisher, except in the case of brief quotations, embodied in reviews and articles.

Cataloguing in publication information is available from Library and Archives Canada.
ISBN 978-1-77458-642-6 (paperback)
ISBN 978-1-77458-743-0 (ebook)

Page Two
pagetwo.com

Page Two™ is a trademark owned by Page Two Strategies Inc., and is used under license by authorized licensees

Cover design by Peter Cocking
Interior design by Cameron McKague

roygroup.net

*To Robert Henderson and Mark Bell
for re-finding the future with me,
as companions,
and introducing me to
this way of being in the world.*

Contents

Foreword by Zita Cobb 1

MEDITATION *In What Way Will You Be Remembered?* 3

Introduction 5

MEDITATION *Something Is Missing* 15

1 **Our Adjacent Worlds** 17

MEDITATION *Be What Is Required Most* 29

2 **Never Call Yourself a Mentor** 31

MEDITATION *Do Not Sidestep Your Work* 45

3 **This Is About Who You Are** 47

MEDITATION *Know What It Is Time For* 55

4 **Are You a Person of Practice?** 57

MEDITATION *Reign Over the Moments of Your Life* 69

5 **The Primacy of Conduct** 71

MEDITATION *Stay True* 89

6 Staying Clear of Pitfalls *91*

MEDITATION *Be Exquisite in Your Execution* *105*

7 The Power of Example *107*

MEDITATION *Notice What Is Being Learned* *121*

8 Focus on Learning, Not Teaching *123*

MEDITATION *Be Judicious with What You Share* *133*

9 Your Advice Is Worth Less (Than You Think) *135*

MEDITATION *Midwife the Triumphs of Others* *147*

10 It's Not About You *149*

MEDITATION *Share Intelligence—Not Niceties* *161*

11 Encouragement Is a Shortcut *163*

MEDITATION *Questions Set Us Free* *175*

12 You Are Not Asking Enough Questions *177*

MEDITATION *Time to Move* *189*

13 Strategy on the Fly *191*

MEDITATION *Share What You Noticed— Not What You Think* *203*

14 Feedback Helps Us Find Our Way *205*

MEDITATION *Move Straight Towards the Pain* *219*

15 We Are Not Built for Easy *221*

MEDITATION *Every Person Has a Gift* *231*

16 The Meaning of Life *233*
(Has Been with You the Whole Time)

MEDITATION *Entangle Yourself in Community* *247*

17 Get It Together, Together *249*

MEDITATION *Be Discerning* *263*

Conclusion: Why I Wrote This Book *265*

MEDITATION *Be Agile in Your Conversations* *267*

Acknowledgements *269*

MEDITATION *Stop Yourself from Interrupting Magic* *275*

Foreword

I FIRST MET Ian Chisholm ("Chiz") when he came as a convenor to the Fogo Island Inn for gatherings of social enterprise leaders and philanthropists. It was not a surprise to me that he was from Saskatchewan. Watching him work, I could tell that he really likes people. He kept the big picture clearly in his mind while tending to details, big and small, that let people know that they were cared for—and cared about. He was focused on development, in the best meaning of the word: "To discover, to advance, to strengthen, to progress, to bring forward." I recognized this in Chiz because our work at the Shorefast Foundation is focused on this meaning of development for communities in the same way that Roy Group is focused on development as it relates to the next generation of leaders within those communities.

During the lockdowns and shutdowns of the COVID pandemic, Chiz reached out with his team to offer support to our senior team as we navigated the crisis. Although virtual by necessity, it proved to be a very useful process. We were thrilled to welcome Chiz back to Fogo for a month in April 2023, for his writing sabbatical. Every morning we saw him in the library at the inn, writing away on his laptop. Every afternoon, Chiz would shift gears to work with one of our teams. And for many of the evenings that April, we were able to have dinner together and discuss the key themes that were emerging in the drafts of this book:

Community is a need and a gift.
Chiz sees the world through the lens of community. The world would be better if we could find more ways to strengthen our communities. We often take it for granted until it has almost been lost. As life becomes increasingly unpredictable, we would be wise to invest in community in any way and as often as we can.

Mentorship strengthens community.
Creating networks of mentors in our communities and our organizations is one way that we can do this. And as Chiz reminds us in chapter 17—we must get it together, together! It is time for us to start positioning our next generation of leaders to be able to do what they will need to do. If this book is in your hands, you are part of the solution.

Mentorship is challenging.
The shift from leadership to mentorship can be challenging. It involves driving a little less hard for results at all costs, and slowing down to create some space for developing the capacity of others. Mentorship uses the language of community, and it moves at the community's pace. This takes patience. It takes setting our own egos aside. It takes generosity. And it takes practice.

The secret is doing it with care.
If you are going to do something, do it with care: care for the work, and for the people who will interact with the work now and in the future. It you do it with care, you will do it well. That shows up in quality, and quality changes lives for those who create it and for those it is created for.

Enjoy the care that went into this book.

Zita Cobb is the founder and CEO of Shorefast Foundation and the first innkeeper of the Fogo Island Inn.

MEDITATION
In What Way Will You Be Remembered?

In what way will you be remembered?
Carved into marble?
Postured tall in bronze?
Looking out over all that you have created
with concentration carefully etched
into your look of ruthless focus?

In what way will you be remembered?
Will we break the code
of your steed's stance
to decipher how you met your end?
Will we read a footnote of when
on the pedestal history has put you on?

In what way will you be remembered?
Will you be with us in the sparks
rising from the big house fire?
Released to reveal our faces

in every moment
the embers are disrupted.

In what way will you be remembered?
As you are drawn
into the dervish dancing
of disappearing up
into the darkness of the night sky
beyond mountains of clouds and thunder.

In what way will you be remembered?
Travelling as we travel
to the place
where all gravity collapses
to ignite again
and be born an overwatching star.

In what way will you be remembered?
We see you now
amongst the many.
Allowing us to know who and where we are.
And the way we must go
to start our next fire.

Introduction

The journey of humanity is the journey from ignorance to enlightenment. It's like an endless march of souls through eternity. If you are standing in an infinitely long line of souls, how can you say that your position is superior to others? When there is no head and no end to the line, it doesn't matter what place you hold.

DENG MING DAO

THE ALARM went off at 4 a.m.

The importance of the day had my subconscious sitting straight up within milliseconds. I felt a tightness in my gut, but wasn't yet awake enough to discern what this day was for. *Why had I set my alarm so early? And why so loud?*

Did I have to cram for a chemistry exam? Was I going skiing?

My conscious mind caught up a few seconds later. My eyes widened. This was the day I would attend an open-heart surgery.

In the final year of my science degree, a quiet champion of mine named Ray Nelson had orchestrated this opportunity. He knew I aspired to get into medical school, and that having an experience like this might give me something to write about in my application essay or mention in an interview.

I arrived at the hospital and was directed to make my way down to the operating theatres. From surgery scenes in TV shows, I was expecting to be sitting quietly above the theatre in a glassed-in observation area. Me and the med students. Maybe a few members of the patient's family.

To my surprise, no such observation area existed. I was gowned and booted and scrubbed up next to the surgical team. Moments later, I found myself standing inches from the patient's head, a man in his early 60s.

Ray had set me up to have the best seat in the house.

The procedure itself was a quadruple bypass, where a large blood vessel taken from the patient's leg is reconfigured to replace key arteries serving the chambers of the heart. That's really all I can tell you. Because surprisingly, my focus wasn't drawn to the mind-bending science of what I was witnessing. Not the pH of the ice being sloshed into an open chest cavity, nor the blood-spurting procedure of sewing vessels into place.

All I noticed—for the nearly four hours I stood there—was an exquisite dynamic between remarkable people. The calm, methodical communication in the monitor-rich corner between the seasoned anaesthesiologist and her student. The careful movements between nurses to supply the senior surgical nurse with the instruments he needed to pass to the surgeon. The care and attention from the veteran surgeon listening to the younger one narrating his thought process and identifying what his next actions would be.

All I could see was the complete investment of time and focus people were giving each other.

In retrospect, the writing on the wall was clear: I wasn't destined to be a doctor. I wasn't focused on that part of it. Instead, I would spend the rest of my life experiencing, noticing and trying to understand human potential—and the relational dynamics that set it free.

Ray's quiet championing had brought me one step closer to my calling—just not in the way either of us was expecting.

This book is an invitation into a special kind of mentorship—an investment of your time, your focus and a deeply cultivated *belief* in others. It is about learning to recognize when unhelpful dynamics surface (they frequently appear in our current understanding of mentorship) and to have something more compelling to anchor to. This book shares some ideas that my mentors and my team have been tending to for decades, and some useful tactics that help mentors raise their game in moments that count. There is no greater joy to experience than the fulfillment that comes from helping honourable people, from all walks of life, to cross the threshold from being leaders to becoming a very special kind of mentor.

Mentor's Way

The origin of the word *mentor* dates back to the ancient Greeks and their love of stories and epic personifications. Specifically, a trio of characters named Telemachus, Mentor and the goddess Athena.

When Odysseus was called to join the Trojan War—a war he was reluctant to engage in—one of his most substantial decisions was whom to position as a role model for his eight-year-old son, Telemachus, while he was away. For any of us who are parents, it's heart-wrenchingly clear how much thought and consideration Penelope and Odysseus must have put into this choice. After serious reflection, Odysseus approached his former teacher and friend, a serious little man named Mentor.

This tender template of a father putting arrangements in place before embarking on a journey he may not come back from would be strategically picked up in 1699 in the publication of *Les Aventures de Télémaque*, a book written by French Catholic archbishop François Fénelon. Fénelon was the specially appointed private tutor to the grandson of Louis XIV, the young Duc de Bourgogne, who was second in line to the French throne. Fénelon's mission: ready this boy to be a king, just in case it's required.

Fénelon began tutoring the young duke when the boy was only seven years old and published *Les Aventures* when the duke turned seventeen. Fénelon was careful to shape the character of Mentor through a lens that positioned himself, as the obvious parallel to Mentor, in a very good light: easy to admire, an exemplar of integrity and gifted in the ability to connect. Writing *Les Aventures* was a shrewd strategy for someone close to power who needed his connection with the teenager to deepen. His depiction of Mentor also popularized the archetype that we're familiar with today.

The only problem was, Fénelon's story left out some key features of the original. Like the fact that the original Mentor had none of these admirable attributes. Mentor's relationship with Telemachus was awkward and strained. There was no spark between them. In his older years, Mentor struggled to connect across the generational gap with Telemachus at all. In fact, the original Mentor made a royal mess of it. In Mentor's presence, Telemachus struggled with insecurity, indecision and a chronic lack of confidence.

Mentor's way *didn't work*.

It's a good reminder for all of us that this path of mentorship might not be exactly what we thought it would be. It is fraught with stumbling blocks and pitfalls—a path where each of us will need to check ourselves often and find a better way forward.

Something else I have taken from this origin story is that Mentor was someone's name. For a long time, I went out of my way to capitalize the word *Mentor* as a proper noun whenever it appeared in my writing. If someone pointed out that I didn't need a capital letter there, I would quietly say, "Yes, I do," and it would give me the chance to tell them the story of where the word comes from. I've given up on that convention, but not the idea. I never use *mentor* as a verb. Not once in this book will you see the word *mentor* with *-ing* at the end of it. Because I don't think it accomplishes as much good in the world as it can when the word changes from being something you do to someone, or even *for* them, and becomes something you *are* to them.

When *mentor* is used as a verb, I'm not exactly sure what the person is describing. I've overheard too many conversations where people are using it to mean different things: For example, one person is referring to sharing technical expertise while the other person is talking about sharing one's experience. They think they're talking about the same doing. They rarely are.

In essence, mentorship is about being an important character in the story of someone's life. Being conscious of this gets us all much closer to the magic. When a person is talking about their experience of mentorship, they are mapping out what it means to be uniquely them, in combination with another original human being. My using *mentor* only as a noun serves as a reminder to me that as a character's name within an epic story, it is a placeholder for yours (and mine).

Athena's Way

Fortunately for Telemachus in the original story, some big-league help in the form of a divine intervention was on its way. The goddess Athena had promised Odysseus that she would watch over and protect his family. When she saw the relationship between Mentor and Telemachus disintegrating, she took action. As Homer described it, "Down the sky she swooped through the clear bright air / Like a shrieking, sharp-winged hawk." And inserted herself into the situation—literally—by taking over Mentor's physical form.

In disguise, Athena wasn't able to use her supernatural celebrity status or her legendary war stories to win Telemachus over. She had only her signature presence and a disciplined way of conducting herself. Which was all she needed to turn the tide. A wise warrior and master weaver was now on the scene, and Athena's compelling way of being captured the young man's attention. She built trust and connection. She adapted to whatever was required. She was patient. She became everything any parent would want their child to have access to. And perhaps most importantly, it really didn't matter to her who got the credit. Her identity was not at stake and her ego was quiet, all for the sake of someone else.

Athena had a strong track record as the champion of courageous endeavours and patron of leaders in a jam. Long before and after Telemachus, it was Athena and her practice of accompanying heroes that established a source of connection, belief and guidance to a long list of storied leaders: Perseus, Bellerophon, Heracles, Jason.

It was Athena's way that made the difference.

I hope the convictions you need the most will stand out as challenging—perhaps ideas you have to sit with for a while.

Her companionship as both a wise strategist and honed practitioner ignited the relationship Telemachus needed. And it steered a potentially disastrous situation to a better place.

Athena's pivotal role as companion and quiet champion is at the very least a reminder that each of us had better be open to forces beyond ourselves in our relationships as would-be mentors. Perhaps these forces will appear in the memories we have of those who were mentors to us. Perhaps they will appear in the form of others who are on this path with us. Perhaps simply aging will change us. Perhaps some form of divine intervention will intercede and steer us all towards connecting properly.

To be clear, this book has no divine powers, but it could provide glimpses of what Athena embodied to create transformational relationships with those she accompanied. It may also shed light on some of the pitfalls that got the original Mentor into such a mess. Learning from both can help us be aware of who the quiet champions have been for us—and guide us to occupying that ground ourselves.

The Choice to Do Something Well

After several years of working for Operation Enterprise, a management development program delivered on college campuses, I wound up taking the post as the first chief executive of the Columba 1400 Community and International Leadership Centre on the Isle of Skye. This important assignment put me in way over my head. Our work on Skye centred on eliciting the leadership potential of young people from Scotland's toughest socio-economic realities. I was 27, a brand-new husband and a brand-new dad. Set in the complex local context of a small, rural island community of 500, our operation and financial requirements were very much of a big-city nature. I did not have the financial or strategic acumen required to be a start-up CEO. As I would find out, what I *did* have was an exquisite network of mentors who would champion me.

One was with me every day. Anne-Marie and I had only been married for six months when we made the move to the Isle of Skye. She had moved many times as a teenager and was well versed in all the things a person needs to do in entering a new community and becoming part of it. She is also a savvy mediator: Her listening skills and ability to understand (even when she doesn't agree) engage people at a very deep level. She is a keen observer of nature's genius and a force of change in any community she is a part of. The Athena Signature—which I'll discuss in more detail in chapter 3—is strong in this one.

In Scotland, I would learn a lot quickly, and I'd make a choice: to always do my best.

To Athena, doing something well was important. And your desire to do the things a mentor needs to do well is probably what landed this book in your hands. With practice, the awkward starts to feel more natural, and the more natural can eventually start to feel exquisite. As this book's author, I want to help embed this pattern in your life and thank you for your desire to do what you do properly—with a heads-up that mentorship is more about being than it is about doing.

Your inclination to pick up this book, and my decision to write it, are both very small steps in the long human journey from one generation to the next. We are tapping into an age-old appetite, hoping to multiply our influence and be part of a much wider and lasting solution. Mentorship is the most ancient and powerful strategy of personal development our planet has ever known. It is an interaction that's so much a natural part of our humanness that we've long underestimated how much the world needs it.

Even though your first few attempts at mentorship might have fallen a bit flat, you recognize there's something worth practising here. You see others who make mentorship look natural. They immediately put others at ease: They know what to say and how to say it, and they take the conversation where it needs to go. And like other times in your life when you've wanted to hone a practice—how to play the guitar, say, or have a great garden—you've arrived at the realization that becoming a mentor is going to take work.

I'd like to invite you to do this work.

This book is a capturing of key patterns at the heart of valuable mentor experiences. These patterns are important for leaders to know as they step into mentorship roles. For some leaders, this threshold appears precisely as they enter into the final chapters of their career. For others, it's a boundary they cross over and back again at different points throughout their career, serving as a mentor to others and also being on the receiving end along the way. In each case, mentorship comes with its own distinct set of constraints, motivations, invitations and pitfalls that are best navigated with a full awareness of the territory, and a collection of tactics up your sleeve. My hope is that the convictions you need the most might stand out as challenging—perhaps ideas you have to sit with for a while. I also hope that many of these perspectives will confirm things that you've sensed, too, even if you've never given voice to them before.

This book will help you choose a selection of behaviours that are helpful and turn the volume down on those that are not. I've also included some of my favourite tactics for amplifying the impact of your conversations with mentees and other mentors. Heeding your appetite to make changes and taking steps to fulfill it will mean a sacrifice of your time, effort and attention, and all kinds of uncomfortable learning and growth.

At the end of each chapter, I invite you to reflect and bring your own story to the table. These questions, I hope, will prompt some deep and honest digging. I want you to feel free to write unpolished thoughts or emotions. That's how reflection works: We put it out there and then figure out what truths lie within it.

Find a journal and pen you enjoy using. And a place you can return to, again and again, that allows you to reflect properly.

I encourage you to write your notes privately, with the kind of courage that comes from trusting that these thoughts won't be shared in their original form. I'd like for you to understand your desire to be a mentor and the motivations that are driving it. Some are true and will endure. Some will fall away. Some of our motivations, if left unchecked, could do damage and hurt people. I'd like to invite Athena's courage, craft, wisdom and humility into the way you take this on. The world around you will benefit because you've done that digging, distilled down your motivations and integrated what you've found.

Stepping onto this path honours those who stepped up for you—people like Ray Nelson, who, in the midst of a demanding day leading his own rapidly expanding lumber company, picked up the phone to arrange for a mediocre science student to get up early, scrub up with a surgical team and get his world rocked.

The best part is, it isn't just who the two parties in a mentor relationship are today, but who they are becoming. Each person embodies a set of distinct qualities that enable the other to evolve towards being more completely themselves, too. When mentors come to understand that it is who they *are* that makes them valuable to the interaction, it all becomes something akin to friendship—and spending time with someone who you enjoy being around.

So let's get you on your way.

REFLECTION

- What are some of the biggest questions you have about your practice of mentorship?

For example:
- What would it look like if I did this really well?
- What would make time with me most valuable?
- How might I signal to others that I would like to play this role?
- Who are some other people who might be ready to practise mentorship with me?

MEDITATION
Something Is Missing

Something is missing.
Your days have been as full as they could be
for as long as you can remember.
But the summer around you and within you
is giving way to a soft chill.
Each evening, it asserts itself a little more.

Something is missing.
You notice the space where it would sit,
not knowing what it is makes it a gnawing gape.
This missing has come from tissues twisting inside,
creating a spirit space that was not there before.
It aches to be known for what it is.

Something is missing.
Unlike the missing when someone is taken away.
Or waking in tears when we dream of them.
As searing as those missings are,
they are not this mystery.
This shape inside our hearts is for those we have not yet met.

Something is missing.
We go inside ourselves to understand the void.
But come up empty.
That is what voids provide.
It is only in the depths of this emptiness
that we realize that others are feeling it, too.

Something is missing.
Everywhere. For everyone.
You need them, and they need you.
Tiny rays of significance and belonging
the only touchpoints where the light of others
can connect you to all that is.

Something is missing.
It is in this space that the finest
self of others can find landfall.
Just as you will find what you are looking for,
by being the signature presence
others have been missing.

I

Our Adjacent Worlds

*I know. I was there. I saw the great void
in your soul, and you saw mine.*

SEBASTIAN FAULKS

MENTORSHIP BEGINS WITH a sense of connection across generations.

We arrive into a family needing to count on others to keep us safe and nourished. We learn that trusting others makes us part of something. I grew up on the Canadian prairies and am a very proud Saskatchewanian. My great-grandma Florence lived in a small house in the corner of our farmyard. My father's parents, Mary and Roy, lived in the big farmhouse in the centre of that yard. We lived across the road; it took less than a minute to be in their kitchen.

In retrospect, it was a remarkable concentration of quiet and hard-working folks from four generations, all living in our little spot under the most wide-open and wild-skied place I have ever known. It created a childhood for my brothers and me that was both magical in its freedom and regimented in its responsibilities. Now that I am older, I can appreciate that it was a unique upbringing and place that provided the chance for me to pay attention to quiet champions all around me, and did so for as long as I can remember.

I remember a conversation with my uncle Ian, whom I'm named after. He listened to me, at age 33, explain all the reasons Anne-Marie and I wanted to name our new company in honour of my grandpa Roy, his father. I talked about how I wanted Roy Group clients to feel the same steadiness and high standards that Roy Chisholm always brought to his work and interactions with others. How he was kind and generous in his understanding of the value in failure when learning new things, and patient when my brothers and I made mistakes on the farm.

Uncle Ian listened for a long time. When I had unpacked everything and laid it out before him, he finally spoke.

"It sounds like your grandpa and my dad were two very different people."

His words stuck with me. They were unfreighted by any resentment or judgment. He said it like it was logical, but with a tone that suggested he was ready to wonder about it with me: *Exactly how does a person's nature evolve across the arc of their life?* The Roy Chisholm my uncle had known as his dad in his 30s, 40s and 50s was a different version of the man in his 60s, 70s and 80s my brothers and I had grown up across the road from. Had Athena intervened? Was this same shift in store for me and my brothers one day? Was Grandpa Roy's shift due to a conscious desire to get things more and more right? Had he wanted to become a mentor? Or was this something that happens naturally from deep wells of potential below the surface?

Perhaps it can be all of these things.

The Void You Feel

Let's talk about what's happening in you as you reach this stage in your career.

More than anything external, I suspect what tipped the balance in leading you to a book about the oldest known method of human development is something really important that's happening inside. And it has some layers.

It starts with some intellectual reasoning:

- You're up for a new challenge.
- You would like to share your hard-won experience.
- You sense that sharing your experience would be valuable to others.
- You believe you could spare others the gut-heave of some dumb mistakes.
- It makes sense for you to be of service.
- You could carve out some time to contribute meaningfully.
- You've been influenced by others stepping up as mentors.

But there's more to it. Underneath that rationale, there's some emotional fuel:

- It feels like the time to give back.
- You're realizing the places where you've carried the most painful experiences in your life have deepened into wells of empathy and compassion for others, ready to be shared.
- You want to let people tackling difficult things know that it's workable—that life is hard, but they're going to get through, somehow.
- You would like to forge some deeper connections with people and be trusted to get below the surface with them.
- You'd like to feel that tearful joy that comes with connection a little more often.

Deeper still, there's something at the level of spirit:

- You're aware that your finest self wants to make its finest contribution.
- You would like to be significant in the lives of others—a paradoxical urge to pass the torch and still be a part of it all.
- There is a part of you that likes the idea of having your photo in the corner of a dojo somewhere, alongside those who have been mentors to you. You would like to be held in high regard.

- You would like to belong to some order of heroic folks who are remembered.
- You feel that, in some way, if you play your cards right, you can find a way of being with people permanently.

Perhaps it's this sharp awareness of our mortality that has made the desire to be a mentor quietly urgent for us. When we fully acknowledge our physical impermanence, we suddenly feel a strange need to get moving. The ticking clock whispers that there's something missing. We are growing older every moment. If ultimately there is good to be done by us, we must begin to find our way. We can feel it in the twisting tissues of our being. It is time for a new and arduous journey to begin.

Zugunruhe is the concept of migration restlessness, from the German *zug* (*to move*) and *unruhe* (*a sneaking anxiety*). It describes the strange and unconquerable urge an animal experiences at the threshold of an inevitable migration. Changing external conditions, like temperature and light, stir a set of changes inside. Switches get flipped—and they can't be unflipped. *Zugunruhe* is not pretty and it is not kind. Organs atrophy to make space for prolonged periods of structural reconstitution. Insatiable appetites build up fat stores. *Zugunruhe* disrupts from the inside out. And the more important the *zug*, the more dramatic the *unruhe*.

I sense a collective human *zugunruhe* will emerge in the next few generations before we are gone. It is inescapable. For so many of us, it starts with some uncomfortable questions about the career we chose. We've experienced being the audacious rookie, starting new things and seeing them through. We've experienced epic wipeouts and recovered. We've experienced success. And yet we still yearn for something more.

We have a sense that what we're looking for we will find in others, across generations and across divisions. We feel the need to be significant in the lives of people who don't yet know us, knowing that this will be the true measure of our value here: that people love us dearly even though the world does not require them to. We yearn for significance, for our brief moment here to be a flame worth protecting, a light worthy of notice, a spark that ignites others before it is gone.

This urge originates from deep inside, honed over millions of years to jolt us out of being absorbed with ourselves and our own achievements.

We might choose to ignore the whispers for a while, but they can't be denied. Something does not feel complete. The doldrums we feel in our own challenges, day after day, create a feeling close to staleness. The discomfort builds. Perhaps we take up a new hobby or begin having coffees with interesting people to fill the void. But they're not the ones we really want to be having coffee with.

It's the future that we're searching for a connection with.

The Void They Sense

The next generation wants to spend time with us, too. They just might not know it.

I cringe a bit hearing generational stereotypes, particularly when they're loaded with judgment and disdain.

"This new generation isn't prepared to put the work in."

"Millennials can't take criticism."

"These Gen Z kids just don't value the sacrifices others have made."

If the next generation is not ready for the challenges they're going to be facing, that's as much on us as on them. Each generation of leaders steps into a totally different context, largely created by whatever the leaders before them built, allowed to be built . . . or failed to build altogether.

Our next generation is walking into a doozy.

They're inheriting an increasingly unpredictable world to live and work in, or lead each other through. Consider the contents of the little gift basket we're handing over:

- climate change and what it means if we cannot change course together
- a breakdown in biodiversity, habitat and the planet's ability to support life
- the widening disparity between economic wealth and poverty
- a tsunami of industry-agnostic private equity buying up what used to be owned by our neighbours
- the mass migration of people due to drought, hunger, persecution and violence
- social media and the psychology of exclusion and bullying
- a resurgence of white supremacy, racism, hate and empire-builders wanting to expand their territory
- loneliness, abuse, intergenerational trauma and addiction
- our inability to govern developing technologies like artificial intelligence and biotechnology
- the simultaneous polarization of politics, media and social networks, and the shenanigans that this is distracting our attention away from

How could they *not* be overwhelmed by a world requiring them to face such wicked and complex dynamics?

The public discourse about topics like these requires an understanding of ethics that we've neglected for decades. This is a world where emerging leaders must notice context over any attachment to easy answers or best practices. They'll need to forge their livelihoods by sidestepping fast-moving threats and rooting out elusive opportunities. Information is flowing in a way it never has before—but it also needs to be highly scrutinized and filtered. Today's world requires the kind of rigorous pattern recognition and rapid sense-making that no single person can do on their own.

This new generation of leaders will have to try multiple strategies to find a few that work. They'll need to lead with great and ever-increasing awareness, focus, creativity, integrity, perseverance and

It is the birthright of the next generation's leaders to be surrounded by a council of the skilled, the willing and the wise.

———————————

service. We can't ask them to lead alone, but when we don't step up to accompany them, that's precisely what we're doing. At exactly the moment when our next generations of leaders need to be connected with us and each other, they are not. And it creates a lot of private suffering for them and for us. Isolation and loneliness have never been as prevalent as they are now as forces shaping the future of society.

Becoming a mentor isn't *our* birthright, as leaders who have reached the zenith of our careers and are now on the gently coasting downslope towards retirement. It is the birthright of those of the next generation who choose to lead: to be accompanied by a council of the skilled, the willing and the wise that is invested in who they are becoming.

I am not a musician, but I've learned from my oldest son, Jameson, about this concept of accompaniment. For professional musicians, a request to accompany is a very specific one. It means there is a role required to support the main performer and assist in bringing their creation to life. *Their* name is on the marquee outside. The crowd will cheer loudest when *they* step out on the stage. *They* will feel the full heat in the centre of the spotlight. They are asking us to support from the shadows—a part of the background to what they unveil. We believe in the potential of whatever unique piece they have prepared, and we come prepared to champion them in performing it.

Accompaniment is a role that requires experience, skill, practice, focus and humility, all wrapped in the package of a generous and attentive companion dedicating themselves fully to what someone else is attempting to create. It is about remaining *with*. It is an act of quiet championing, and being like Athena was: not needing status, applause or recognition.

Being accompanied displaces the anxious void they feel.

It will fill the one that we've been sensing, too.

The Challenge We Share

The impact that mentorship can have on our society comes from two primary sources. It provides a network of good governance around the choices being made by an emerging generation of leaders: students, rookies and audacious young upstarts. It also provides a source of meaning, engagement and significance for those with a lifetime of experience and insight: seasoned veterans, community champions and folks shifting into a different phase with some time on their hands.

But like a chemical reaction, it takes contact and connection with all kinds of characters to stir up this potential. It requires multiple, frequent and substantial collisions. It requires the language of community, where people say the things that initiate ties to each other, and where they create opportunities to spend more time together:

"There are some people I'd like you to meet having breakfast together."

"We're grabbing a coffee on Wednesday. Can you come?"

"I'd love it if you could bring me up to speed on what you have been working on."

The challenge we share is that community is a disappearing way of life. And yet, the magic of mentorship is found squarely within the realm of community—where cousins, grandmothers, aunts, neighbours and elders reside. Where store clerks and librarians do their work. Where bus drivers and vice-presidents and foresters show up, week after week.

Community is how mentorship happens—even when it's taking place in more "official" realms like education, business or government.

Education, business and government have ways of sustaining themselves to be strong, relevant and permanent. We expect people within these sectors to make decisions in line with this and to do what they need to do. They develop mechanisms for making good choices and contingencies for tough times. There is a focus on risks and rewards. Good outcomes are easily measured or monetized. And, of course, there are leaders who are motivated to steer things well. Watch a principal, a CEO, an activist or an elected official move a priority that they've bet their job on, and you'll see what it looks like to show up and lead.

Outside of these worldly sectors, communities have had similar ways of sustaining themselves—but these ways are deteriorating at a rate greater than they're being strengthened. Our sense of place is being lost faster than the technological promise to actually connect us is being realized.

The dawn of so-called social media made all kinds of promises. *People who share a passion will be able to find each other and make things happen!* That ended up being both a blessing and a curse. What it actually provided was a way for each of us to find the 50 percent of the people across the planet who agree with us—not the people we're *actually* in community with, but the ones we have to figure out a way forward with. What social media can't do is be a place. It can't drop off a tray of lasagna on the step of a neighbour who's just lost a family member in a car accident. It can't rebuild the barn after a tornado. It can't swing by and take your kids to soccer practice to save you the trip.

Community provides the chance for us to gather and notice each other *in situ*. To notice if someone has begun to struggle, or recover. To notice if someone else is starting to lead, or might be available to us as a resource—maybe even as a mentor. It allows us to experience and share in the food we eat here, the songs we sing here and the way we say things here. It's a place where we have to take accountability for what we say because we're going to run into each other at the grocery store.

It is in community gathering that we understand the place we are from—the place we are *of*. The place where we will be buried or have our ashes scattered. These gatherings provide the only way that visitors can gain a sense of what it really means to be "from this place."

Some communities still have very strong ways. I've found that these are often communities with their back against the wall. Small prairie towns and island villages fighting to protect their livelihoods and ways of life, up against a threat and hanging by a thread. Or remote Indigenous communities indefatigably overcoming centuries of adversity and trauma, and protecting their language, their songs, their dances and their culture to create a forward path of healing.

In these communities, the thought that we don't need each other is incomprehensible.

It is most notably when a community is vulnerable to being lost that it suddenly realizes its own value. This value is difficult to measure or monetize, which is why I sense we ignore it until it's almost gone before realizing in astonishment that it's worth fighting for. Most of us fail to see community as an equal pillar to government and business. Because it isn't equal.

It's worth more.

Community underpins everything else. Government and enterprise don't function properly without it. When either of them loses its healthy connection to community, we see things spin into chaos. Show me a school, a business or a political body that gets itself into some serious trouble, and I will point out their disconnect from the community.

It's impossible to overestimate the power of community as mentors. It is what our efforts as mentors are ultimately building.

REFLECTION

- What are your reasons for wanting to be a mentor?
- What is your relationship to community?

MEDITATION
Be What Is Required Most

Be what is required most.
When it is time to step in,
give all of your attention to whatever is in front of you.
Distill your intention to answer the call.
Meet the moment with agility,
choosing silently to be what is needed most.

Be what is required most.
When it is time to be an example,
choose to be transcendent.
Give people a performance
that makes them want to stand and cheer,
and tell stories of it to everyone they love.

Be what is required most.
When it is time to instruct,
choose to make the lesson indelible.
Ignite each idea like a torch
to carry forward
into the night.

Be what is required most.
When it is time to advise,
choose to be spartan with your offering.
Select the one piece of advice
you know will make the biggest difference,
and leave the rest for another time.

Be what is required most.
When it is time to invite the potential of others
onto the field of play to shine,
choose to engage the process with all your heart
and embody the spirit of the endeavour
from the sidelines and the shadows.

Be what is required most.
When it is time to champion,
choose to be an invisible force
of belief, of connection and of opportunity.
Carefully move the least number of pieces required
to set the stage for another's greatness.

2

Never Call Yourself a Mentor

*Let discernment be your trustee,
and mistakes your teacher.*
T.F. HODGE

BOB CHARTIER is a mentor of mine. I share Bob with thousands of public servants and community members across Canada whom he has introduced the practice of engagement to. One of Bob's gifts is his ability to animate stories—like one he had read about a college student walking through the crisp morning air in Vermont.

The community was quiet, in the way only a college town early on a Saturday morning can be, and the student was making his way through the streets to his professor's house. He was showing some extra initiative, taking his professor up on an invitation to talk more about his work.

He knocked and waited for just long enough that he began to doubt if he had the time right. *Maybe this wasn't the right address? Maybe he'd got the day wrong?*

But then the door opened.

Across the threshold appeared the formidable and untamed eyebrows of the poet laureate Robert Frost. He invited his student to come in for a cup of tea, as planned.

The young man seated himself at the kitchen table. He pulled his papers out of his leather fold, eager to not waste the professor's time—although the professor gave no indication of impatience. Small talk and tea preparation. Until the moment arrived.

The young man knew this was his opportunity to begin—to move to the agenda for this meeting. To bare his soul.

"Like you, sir," he ventured, "I am a poet. And I was hoping that you could take a look at some of the things I've—"

The professor held up his hand.

The words died in the young man's throat. The air in the kitchen stopped moving, and an awkward pause descended.

"You can't call yourself that, son."

"I'm sorry, sir?"

"You called yourself a poet."

The student swallowed uncomfortably.

"I have a rule," the professor continued, "that one cannot call themselves a poet. The word *poet* is a gift word. Someone gifts it to you. When they read what you've written and are so moved—it is up to them, and only them, to say that the person who wrote this is, indeed, a poet."

The Gift Words

All of the right people are nodding right now.

They know where I'm going with this and like the idea of *mentor* being a gift word. Even deeper, if you're a person who likes the idea of earning a title rather than just taking it on, this book is really for you. My hope is that this way of using the word feels strangely new but also similar to the way you approach your life.

Gift words are important. They dare us to be discerning and careful about the way we use language. Gift words allow us to change mental models and to accomplish more good in the world by bringing some rigor to how we hold concepts and how we say things.

And gift words are all around us, if we pay attention.

It's certainly fashionable to proclaim that *integrity* is a value one holds dear, but perhaps others have the best perspective to determine whether someone is, in fact, a person of integrity. We can certainly choose to practise leadership and the responsibility and sacrifice that come with it, but perhaps it serves us all well if we are careful when applying the word *leader* to ourselves. And maybe others looking in on the way we play for each other are in the best position to say whether we are a *team*.

Mentor is, quite possibly, the most self-awarded gift word of all time. Thus, it is a word I would like to reclaim and reposition in the very special place in which it belongs in our language: on the top shelf, where the gift words are kept.

When someone uses the word *mentor* to describe the role you're playing (or have played) in their life, it's an important moment. Be conscious of the power that moment holds and what it means. It's an acknowledgement that you matter to them. It's an acknowledgement that they wouldn't be who they are, or where they are, had you not criss-crossed paths with them. It reflects a long series of good instincts on your part for what it was time for, and the initiative you took to step up for them in precisely the way the situation demanded.

So never call yourself a mentor.

It's tacky. It tells me that you're in this for quick hits of social status and admiration.

Catch yourself when you're about to say it and remember that it's a gift word. Notice the opportunity for that word to mean more and accomplish more. If you catch yourself saying it, take it back. Get back to earning it.

Notice how others use the word. You don't need to correct them. Just notice. And recognize the difference.

This is the power of designed constraint—when we bring rigor to how we use, and refuse to use, certain words. Some words may become more meaningful when we self-impose thoughtful constraints. Some important ideas may become more accessible to us and to the world if they are constructed with these honed definitions.

This idea of a gift word, as something that is earned, invites accountability. It invites accountability for where one is putting their attention, for one's actions, and for the relationship with their mentees, and it leads to tending that relationship as one might tend an important friendship. And that is when the magic happens.

For over thirty years, I've asked people this double-barrelled question: "Who is someone who's earned the word *mentor* in your life? And what was it about them that earned it?"

I've had a very small percentage shrug their shoulders and tell me they've never really had a mentor. Or that they learned a little from everyone they've ever met. Some tell stories about people who they learned how *not* to lead from (which I understand).

Sometimes, as the conversation deepens, they change their mind and remember someone they hadn't thought about in a long time.

The vast majority of people, however, are reflective for a moment and then light up. Some know immediately who they want to talk about. Others can't choose and instead share multiple examples of people who have earned the word. There is palpable emotion in their stories. Their descriptions of people are clear and poignant.

Sometimes it's about how they met. We hear stories of first impressions: too abrasive, too abrupt, too good to be true... but over time proven to be the real deal. Sometimes they are relationships that have lasted a lifetime, or people talk about a person they cannot imagine being without. In other stories, mentors are transitory characters who were there at the right place at the right time, but now their whereabouts are unknown. Some relationships even ended in a rupture, a betrayal, a downfall. But people still can't imagine the story of their lives without these characters as part of it all.

Many talk about a parent who overcame terrible circumstances. Or a grandparent who created a new life for their family by moving to another country. Former athletes talk about pivotal coaches who lifted their team to a level of performance, learning and engagement that they didn't think was possible, often by aiming at something bigger than winning. Some talk about first bosses, people who were hard on them, but emphasize that the rigor came from a place of care.

Quite often we hear, "They saw something in me that I didn't sense in myself."

When People Tell Us Their Stories

When people tell stories about their mentors, they'll often talk about just watching them in action. The way they tackled uncomfortable conversations, the way they'd win people over and influence the outcome of a challenging interaction, the way they treated people with power (and people without it) and who they were when their character was tested. It's obvious that part of this journey will be about choosing what you'll be an example of. The importance of being an example is addressed in more depth in chapter 7.

Another subset of stories emerges about their mentors' exceptional instruction. How they would grab a marker and map things out on a whiteboard: a process, an approach, a model. When they chose to share a concept, it was as if they were introducing their protégé to an old friend who would now be in their network. Something critical was being relayed. And whatever it was they were teaching that day has stayed with people the rest of their lives. What was learned from them was indelible. The importance of great instruction is detailed in chapter 8.

There are similar stories about advice. Lots of stories about careful listening and discernment. Quality over quantity. There are not a lot of stories about folks who know it all and hit you with ten pieces of advice twenty seconds into the conversation. I've heard mentees say things like:

- "By the time the advice came, it had been polished just for me."
- "It came as a critical tip at the last possible moment. Stepping into the breach to pull me out of harm's way or to nudge me into an opportunity I was trying to be coy with."
- "What they advised was highly relevant, respectfully and thoughtfully offered."

The importance of advice will be covered in depth in chapter 9.

And there is a cluster of stories about coaching: all of the ways a mentor positioned a mentee for a moment of performance. How they conducted themselves in a way that made mentees feel safe, making risk and innovation possible. Preparing them thoroughly so that they would be confident in the moment that counts. Allowing them to immerse themselves in the challenge without interruption or interference, finding flow and inviting their potential to come out and play. Reviewing their progress with them—leaving no stone unturned—with honest and specific feedback that made them hungry to attempt again and be even better. These mentors had a system for working with people, and it made those people better, allowed them to learn deeply and engaged their souls in the effort. The importance of mentors' coaching is addressed in chapters 12, 13 and 14.

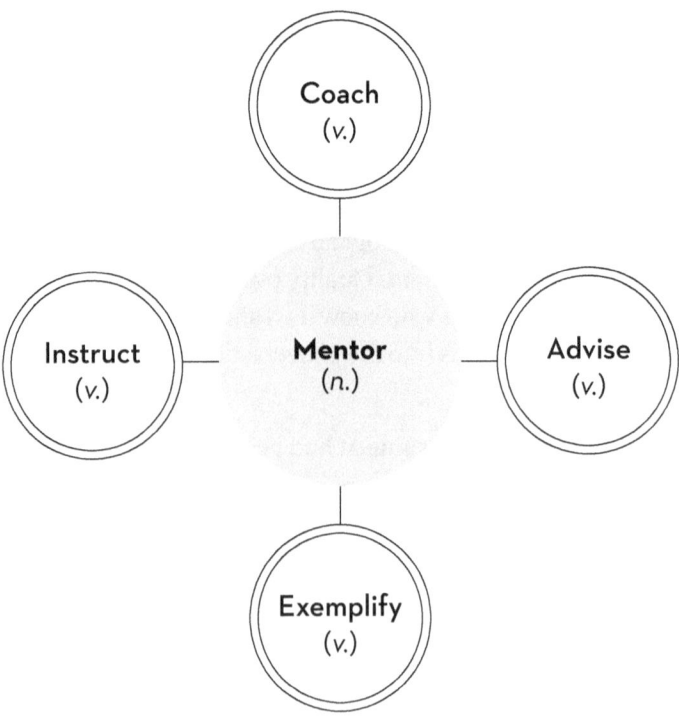

Looking back at our own experiences, we can see that our mentors challenged us. They were often the most honest person in the room. They connected us to the ideas we would need to understand. They pushed us. They told us when we were acting small, snivelling and feeling sorry for ourselves. They pointed out where we needed to raise our game. They supported us, reaching out in moments when we were inconsolable. They offered us a lifeline when we felt we were going under. They connected us to opportunities that would conspire to elicit our most courageous endeavours.

Whatever the situation, they somehow knew what gear to be in.

Don't Grind the Gears

My most prized possession is a 2000 Land Rover Defender 110 named Argento, the Italian word for *silver*. It's a reference to the name of the Lone Ranger's white horse, not the amount of money I put into having Argento run reliably (although both are relevant).

Argento has a storied history that began in Italy, where she was first driven off a lot. She has an expedition sticker from the South Pole on the rear passenger corner and a "Land Rover Ecologica" decal on her back door. At some point, she made her way to Montreal and then across Canada to me. If you saw Argento, you would look twice. She is basic, boxy, bad-ass and beautiful.

Argento drives more like a tractor than a truck. When I first bought her, changing gears was something that took some serious intention. I would find myself looking down to the gear map to remind myself which gear I was in, and where the one I wanted to shift into was. The low-gear and differential options were even more dizzying. In the early days, I would whisper to myself (and to Argento) explicitly what I was attempting to do. It was a little bit clumsy.

A mentorship relationship feels the same to me. I know deep down that it is ultimately about my confidence in sensing what it is time for. When is it time to instruct, to advise or to shift to a coaching approach? When is it time to introduce a person to someone else they need to talk to? Is this the time to support or time to challenge? When do I help the person prepare for a moment that counts? Should

I slow the conversation down now and act like we have all the time in the world, even though I know the clock is ticking? When do I bring urgency to the actions in front of someone? Should I be honest about what I sensed in a moment this person has just come through? When is it time for me to just be there, a quiet and determined force in their corner?

I'm going to need different gears to navigate this terrain. And each gear I'll need is one clear choice. Crunchy noises happen if I'm hesitant or make half-choices. If I can learn to meet each moment with whichever gear is required, the relationship can go wherever it needs to go and create some epic adventures.

It really is a matter of practice. Knowing what explicit options I have and how they are different from each other. What each choice creates and what it thwarts. What conditions need to exist for a certain tactic to work.

After a decade together, driving Argento is strangely automatic. It is a confluence of the sounds the engine is making, the vibrations in the steering wheel and in my seat, what I notice about the conditions in front of me and the momentum we have. I don't look down anymore—I reach and I shift. I don't have to even think about it.

The metaphor of driving Argento is a fun one for me, mostly because Argento is capable of going where many other vehicles are not. I like the spirit of that: No matter where we start from or where we're going, our partnership can get there, as long as we take good care of our vehicle and pay attention to each set of conditions we encounter. There's (almost) always a way forward if we heed the context around us. If we ignore it, confident that the way we roll is going to get us through anything, we're likely going to get ourselves in all kinds of trouble.

TACTIC **Engaging Metaphors**

Sometimes when a person is really digging deep to describe what they're facing, they'll reach for a metaphor (in the same way I just told you about Argento). Everyday language just can't quite describe all the layers and nuances they need to convey. Often without knowing they're doing it, they'll take the conversation into the realm of symbol, where one thing represents another. A metaphor allows the listener to instantly grasp a deeper, richer meaning and to experience the feeling behind a concept. This might be a direct, bold statement:

Mentee: This entire project is a train wreck.
Mentor: A train wreck. Sounds like there's been some damage?

Or it might be slightly more nuanced:

Mentor: Have you noticed that you used the word *battle* twice, *brutality* three times and just said that people are being "hammered down." Could you explain more about your experience with this?

Someone using a metaphor is expressing a desire that the listener fully understand all the unique complexities of an evolving situation. We should pay attention and reflect it back into the conversation.

Alternatively, you could introduce the possibility of simile. If someone is struggling to explain what they're addressing in a way that captures all of the nuance it holds, mentors are wise to ask a question that leaves a wide space for the mentee to fill in.

Mentor: What is this like?

Or:

Mentor: It's as if this is . . . ? (and let the mentee finish the thought.)

Knowing What It Is Time For

Athena would have been highly aware of two concepts of time familiar to ancient Greek society, each with their own distinct personifications.

Chronos represented time as a resource. He was a serious character with a serious message: "There's a limited amount of time and it's running out on us all." Later depicted as Father Time, he held an hourglass as a sober reminder. Chronos is built into our watches and phones as a standard feature. He is in our schedules

In this moment,
with this person, what is
required of me?
_____

and appointment reminders. He loves an efficient and cyclical use of time to get things done.

To Chronos, it is as if we are each walking along a ribbon of time, the past behind us and the future in front of us. When we look down at our feet, the ribbon shows that someone has broken up time into measurable bits: seconds, minutes, hours, days, months, quarters, years and decades. Chronos is the architect of our work ethic, and whispers questions to us constantly, like:

"Is this a productive use of time?"

"When will this need to be done?"

"How much time will that take?"

"What time is it, now?"

Chronos keeps things moving. But to be honest, listening to him for too long can become a bit tedious.

Kairos is a very different personification of what philosophers referred to as "deep time"—which is more about *timing* than time itself. Kairos senses what's happening in front of him and is quick to act when the conditions are right. Kairos is all about the fleeting moment of opportunity: the right time to release the spear, the right time to pass the shuttle through the loom, the right time to reach out and grab a child's hand. This is the kind of time understood at a cellular level by the hunter, the weaver, the parent and, most importantly, mentors who want to develop others as leaders.

Kairos doesn't pester us with questions about how we are using our limited time. He really only has one question, and it's invaluable to anyone who wants to be a mentor:

"What is it time *for*?"

In this moment, with this person, what is required of me?

When it is time to instruct, shift clearly into the gear of skillful instruction. Let the person know you are convinced that learning something new from you is what they need to move forward at that moment. Carve out the appropriate amount of time you will need to share a concept, a model, a process. Draw it out. Walk people through it. Explain why it's best done this way. Answer their questions and help them understand how they can use it. Create an experience that people can continue to learn from the rest of their lives, and pass on to others.

When it is time to shift into advice mode, provide the most articulate, valuable and memorable advice you can muster. Distill it down from the fifty things you *want* to say to the one thing that's most important, and deliver it in a way that will move people. Steer people away from danger and towards opportunity. Help them identify who they need to go and speak with.

When it is time to coach—to use your ability to position someone else for performance—shift gears into that mode. Engage with them and focus on them. See their potential before they do. Have a way of conducting conversations that gets their head in the game and re-establishes what is most important to them. Have a system for clarifying what needs to happen next. Have a method for watching them perform and providing them with feedback. Help people learn from their experience as it emerges.

When it is time to be an example, be exquisite in your choice of something important. Suggest in advance that this is something people may want to take notes on. Choose to be an example and occupy the ground with that mentality. Know that you are being an example as you do something, beautifully. Be your finest self and make your finest contribution.

Don't grind the gears. Don't half-ass what your instinct tells you it is time for. Step up and notice what is around you. When the context tells you what is required, provide it.

Show up ready to offer what people need.

REFLECTION

This is a reflection I've used for decades. I've used it with leaders needing to identify their next moves, and with mentors wanting to know what they need to do next with their mentees. And they have in turn used it to help their mentees find the right action (which I'll discuss more in chapter 4).

1. Place a pen at the top of a clean piece of paper in your journal. Write the question, "What is it time for?"
2. If you get to the question mark and no answer comes to mind, write the question again on the next line.
3. Keep writing this question until you start answering it.
4. Then let yourself write and write and write until you can't write any more.
5. Read through what you have written. Notice your response. Underline what you know is most important.
6. Order your thoughts.
7. Take action.

MEDITATION
Do Not Sidestep Your Work

Do not sidestep your work.
What you are creating in this moment
comes from a long line of story,
sacrifice and risk.
There is no faking this until you make it.
Only facing it—until it is made.

Do not sidestep your work.
Your work is not something you should do.
It is something you must do.
This is the force within you
brought to bear over the distance you have travelled.
Entangle every fibre of yourself with it.

Do not sidestep your work.
Make every sentence, every movement,
every interaction a chance to refine yourself further.
Accept, with all your heart,
that the most important piece of work
you will ever do, is you.

Do not sidestep your work.
Of deepening their capacity.
The tasks, the challenges, the game
are all just opportunities to
refine them further.
Beyond what you yourself have ever accomplished.

Do not sidestep your work.
Shaping the conditions
to invite excellence out to play.
Preparing yourself to be surprised
by just how gifted
someone else's child can be.

Do not sidestep your work.
Rise early to tend to the soil,
and carefully plant the seeds.
Then surrender to exactly how
potential will show itself,
in this beautiful and temporary unfolding.

3

This Is About Who You Are

To be yourself in a world that is constantly trying to make you something else is the greatest accomplishment.

RALPH WALDO EMERSON

WHEN I first heard the simple expression *you are the work*, it seemed innocent enough. It sounded true to me—but not in a way that would commit me to any sort of massive change.

Being in the field of leadership development, I often remind clients and team members that in addition to the demands of our jobs—meetings, tasks, assignments, projects—it is wise to build in some time to work on ourselves: learn something new, challenge ourselves, express something creatively or even just take time to read, reflect or rest. It is pretty clear that mentors play a role in helping our mentees work on themselves.

But it is more than that.

You Are the Work

You are the work is one of those phrases that keeps beckoning at you until the penny drops. It's more than a comfortable nudge. The word *the* is a major clue that there might be some mental model-shifting that needs to happen. Taking a phrase like *you are the work* on board really changes how we see ourselves in relation to the work we do.

When you fully inhabit the phrase, it means you are *the* most important piece of work you will ever be responsible for. Any of those things we thought were "the work"—like your inbox, a new proposal or your next strategic plan—are really just applications of who we are.

Every meal with our families becomes an opportunity to connect deeply with others. Every meeting becomes a chance to be conscientious and to keep our word, fully—even in the presence of time and cost constraints. If we need to renegotiate a deadline or a commitment, the way we do that is something we can take pride in. Every assignment becomes a chance to take on new information and sharpen our ability to make things happen. Every project is a chance to strive for a masterpiece. Every crisis is a chance to demonstrate poise under pressure. Every exchange with the bus driver or the custodian is a chance to create community. And *you are the work* itself provides an opportunity for us to be more fully who we are. Practice is life.

Some think *you are the work* sounds too self-centred and self-serving. They may be nervous about mentors who introduce this idea to our next generation of leaders. After all, this sort of mental model means we are more important than the jobs we hold or the organizations we work for. And that is heresy of the highest order. If our emerging leaders buy into this narcissism, the work will surely suffer. The world will surely suffer. Or will it?

Many of the current mental models that shape how work gets done uphold overextension, personal compromise, imbalance and self-sacrifice. So before you disregard the idea that investing deeply in yourself and your own well-being is the highest priority, take a look at the quality of work that would come about if a focus on self were the central commitment of every person:

- Team members would be accountable for their work products, on time and on budget.
- People would have an appetite for learning of their own choosing and making themselves more valuable.
- Individuals would seek out feedback and use it to strive for finer and finer results.
- People would begin to choose challenges worthy of who they are.
- Every meeting between you and your mentees would create some new awareness or choice.

When individuals working this way come together, what happens in that community is more mindful, principled and deeply meaningful work. Which is just what the world needs more of.

This four-word mantra is a good one to keep up your sleeve. *You are the work* reminds us that our role as mentors is to help others realize that they, themselves, are the most important piece of work they will ever undertake—and the best way for them to realize that is to experience us doing that same work on ourselves right alongside them.

Our true work is to share our most authentic and potent self: that unique essence we brought into the world at the moment of our birth. I call this re-finding my finest self. To this core we add our finest human attributes, evolved over time through exposure to the friction of life's challenges. Our potential is held by this self and shared when the conditions inside us are ready and those around us require it. It's the part of us that invites our physical form into flow state, our intellect to the edges of intuition, imagination and genius, and our emotional state into belonging and community. It is our finest self. It is the part of us that loves. And that is the most important work we will ever do.

Continuity and Improvement

Kaizen is the Japanese concept of continuity and improvement, and is used in business to describe the tradition and disciplines of process design and redesign. Within an ordered system, this approach allows people to design and refine processes that move from inputs (like auto parts) to desired outputs (like an automobile).

As this assembly takes place repeatedly over time, workers who are close to the assembly line notice opportunities to eliminate unnecessary cost, time and frustration. The process gets better and better, and creates more and more of the desired outputs: high-quality cars made cheaper, faster and with less frustration. This is the heart of continuous improvement and appeals to lean, mean efficiency gurus worldwide.

In more unpredictable realms such as human development, the components of continuity and improvement can dance together in a slightly different way. How can something both become better and remain the same? Imagine a flower within its bud, ready for the conditions that will allow it to unfold and become everything it was meant to be.

I find this second interpretation of continuity and improvement much more helpful for the work of mentors and their orientation towards the development of themselves and their mentees. How can I help this person in front of me become more and more of who they have always been?

The Athena Signature

So what was it, specifically, that Athena possessed that Mentor was missing? What is at the crux of what this book is asking each of us to notice in our interactions and begin to practise? It is a pattern that shows up again and again in the actions of impactful mentors and is often the key aspect missing in stories of mentorship relationships that come to an end. I call it the Athena Signature.

The Athena Signature is the paradoxical combination of high self-awareness (knowing one's self deeply) and a disciplined ability to stay focused on the emerging experience of someone else. It allows mentors to put leaders in the centre of their own lives, a task that requires patience, understanding and generosity. It's about catching ourselves giving in to momentary feelings that we have something to prove or a chance to impress, and choosing instead

The word **mentor** also allows us to measure leadership—something that otherwise is very elusive to measurement.

to do the finest thing we can for someone else. Our ability to cultivate self-awareness will allow an endless supply of these instructive, quietly discerning moments to unfold. In each one lies a wonderful invitation to return to occupying the moment as our finest and most essential self and returning our focus to what others are facing.

Stepping up as a mentor in the world takes resolve: *I am going to offer my practice, and who I am, to those who need it. I will shift, adapt, grow and do whatever I can to serve.* This resolve is combined with the humble awareness that I will not be everyone's cup of tea. And that humility allows me to step back, bow out and make enthusiastic referrals to others.

The Measure of Your Leadership

The word *mentor* also allows us to measure leadership—something that otherwise is very elusive to measurement. Some would look at the number of people within a given enterprise, the population of a country or the size of an operational budget. Some would argue there are definable practices that we see demonstrated frequently by those who lead well; we can loosely measure that frequency. Some would argue that to measure a leader, we must wait until the end of a person's career or life to quantify their accomplishments and legacy. At the ends of careers or lives, we often reflect qualitatively on the unique and challenging situations where someone revealed their true character.

To these I would add the number of times a person earns the word *mentor* as a key indicator of someone's ability to lead. Every time that word is gifted to someone, it signals that the person has balanced their own responsibilities with the intensive, focused and demanding work of developing the character, capacity and potential of others. The number of people who refer to you as a mentor in the story of their lives is a reflection of just how many people your heart is capable of caring for: the ultimate metric for any of us who have chosen leadership in our lives.

One other thing I've noticed: the response that true quiet champions have to the moment when someone refers to them as a *mentor*.

They accept the gift with gratitude and find an authentic way to acknowledge that something important has been said. And then—more than pride or celebration or any revelling in the fact that they've earned it—they tuck the gift away out of public sight. It's as if this very special moment is in some humbling mathematical proportion to all of those who were a mentor to them. They feel honoured to accompany.

TACTIC **Resetting the Bead of Focus**
This tactic is a private one, a ritual you can use within your consciousness to move into the Athena Signature state.
Notice.
Notice what you are *aware* of most. Around you. Within you.
Where is there activity? Where is there stillness?
What thoughts occupy the most space, here?
What emotions occupy the most space, here?
What intuitions occupy the most space, here?
How do you occupy this space, here?

———————————

NOW NOTICE where your *focus* has landed.
What has drawn the bead of your attention the most?
What thoughts? What emotions? What intuitions?
Whose thoughts, emotions and intuitions are these?
No judgment; only noticing.

———————————

MOVE THE bead of your attention to rest in the experience of the person you are with.
Their thoughts. Their emotions. Their intuitions.
What is their experience?
Now, ask yourself: "I wonder how they will move through their experience?"

REFLECTION

- Who is someone from the story of your life who embodied the Athena Signature?

MEDITATION
Know What It Is For

Know what it is time for.
The self-whispered question at the core of my dilemma.
Not to be answered from what you think—or even feel.
The answer comes from everything you have sensed
and now know.
Trust what happens next.

Know what it is time for.
If it is time to reflect,
and there is too much to comprehend,
immerse yourself—uninterrupted and uncompromised
until the moment you can see
the nature of what you face.

Know what it is time for.
If it is time to inquire,
then craft the beautiful question
that cracks open what has been locked away
by our fear, our doubt, our hubris
and reverses our submission to the status quo.

Know what it is time for.
If it is time to pause,
do so completely.
Let every cell of your being rest
and settle clear. Be empty.
Feel your momentum come to zero.

Know what it is time for.
If it is time to take action,
act unhindered by hesitation.
Be the words you speak. Be the samurai's sword.
Striking with nothing more
and nothing less than is required.

Know what it is time for.
Whisper this question to the heart of *their* responsibility.
Initiate their practice of the four.
Help them to trust what they know.
When the world needs them to be masterful
it will be too late to start practising.

4

Are You a Person of Practice?

*Practise yourself, for heaven's sake,
in little things, and then proceed to greater.*
EPICTETUS

MENTORS NEED to be practitioners of leadership themselves. The situations your mentee is tasked to lead through will be different from what you faced. The late-night crisis, the merger going sideways, the difficult negotiation—each is a one-of-a-kind context that needs to be explored and understood as such. It's important to not get snagged by the details of your own story. This is about *their* story. But like Athena, that sense you have inside—the knowing in your gut what it feels like to hold responsibility, to come up short of expectations, to have your mettle tested yet rise to the occasion—is an important resource to draw from in our work with leaders.

Mentors need to have been in the fire of it themselves. As much as what you're doing at this very moment is valuable, books on the topic of leadership and mentorship aren't going to get us there. Both leaders and their mentors need to know themselves well enough that they have something to be true to. There may be an abundance of theories about leadership—but it is ultimately not theoretical. There may be lots to study on it—but it is not academic. A person may be a subject matter expert in their field—but leadership is not an expertise. It is a practice. Or more accurately, a set of practices that we learn from fellow practitioners.

We all learn most from our own experience, from finding ourselves in situations where we're in over our heads. We somehow find our feet. We take a good look around. We find some courage. We find the confidence to practise leadership. We establish credibility and find a way forward with others.

And then we reflect on the lessons from our experience. If we are conscious in our reflection, we learn about life, and we learn about our leadership. We learn where our leadership was strong and where it needs some work. It refines us for the next time. The choice to lead is a choice to practise. Whether in their personal lives or as part of a team, an organization or a community, how conscious people are in their practice will determine their impact.

And mentors help people become conscious of the leadership they are practising.

One key way to understand our role as mentors is not just as witnesses but also as catalysts to this cycle of learning from experience. If we can help leaders recognize their leadership as a deepening practice and learn how to approach it with confidence, we'll be helping them extract meaning and growth from every event. The more we help them learn from their experience in this way, the more confident they will be to practise again—and the more their potential as a leader will show itself.

This requires that mentors are people of practice, too. One of the most powerful ways we can accompany people is by practising alongside them. Which is something mentees will immediately recognize in you—that you are a person who is still experiencing life as an opportunity to work on their leadership.

The single most surprising finding in our research into mentorship was about this recognition: When asked to identify when they sensed the value of a relationship with a mentor, the vast majority of mentees said "immediately." Other responses they could have chosen were "after some reflection" or "it's only now that I realize how valuable this relationship was."

It would seem that mentees can instinctively tell when someone has been preparing themselves to be a resource. It's as if at the moment of meeting, any leader is subconsciously asking themselves a few key questions to filter out dead ends:

- *Is this a person who has worked on themselves?*
- *Is this a person still working on themselves?*
- *Does this person have space for me?*
- *Is this person prepared to contribute to my becoming what I could become?*

Mentors need to cultivate within themselves a genuine and generous presence that allows the answer to each of these questions to be a strong and clear "yes." The promise of mentorship is kept through practising *with*. And when we meet these people in our lives, we never forget them.

Mentees can instinctively tell when someone has been preparing themselves to be a resource.

———————

Over two decades ago, I met Robert Henderson through my work in Scotland. Robert has a big, wide smile and speaks with conviction. A colleague of Robert's named Steve Mostyn had read about the work we were doing on the Isle of Skye with young people from difficult socioeconomic conditions and wanted to drive up, have a coffee and find out more about our approach. When I found out Steve and Robert were based outside Glasgow, I let them know that it was a five-hour drive up to Skye, and that maybe a phone call would make more sense for them. But they knew how far away the island was and were still keen to come for a coffee.

I'm very grateful that they did. I liked them immediately.

Robert explained that he was preparing to step out of corporate life; he was serving as senior vice-president of leadership and learning at Motorola for an area including Africa, the Middle East and Europe. Steve helped me understand just how many leaders around the world Robert had helped to practise as leaders—and that I would be wise to consider some way of getting Robert involved with what we were doing.

Steve was right: Robert epitomizes what a quiet champion is. The Athena Signature is woven into everything he does. Above all else, he is a kind companion. He is patient and understanding, but also ready to talk about what's getting in the way of your potential. There's a vitality and an energy that brim from within—something he nurtures and takes care of. He's designed a ready creativity in himself. He's happy to try something new while making a very conscious choice to deepen those practices that he most wants to shape his life.

There is a reason why this book is dedicated to him.

I have learned more about mentorship from Robert than anyone I've ever met. One of Robert's original concepts, which Roy Group affectionately refers to as Henderson's Disciplines, is something I first saw scratched out on a pad of yellow paper. It was a framework Robert had been working on in his last months of corporate life that addressed these questions: "What were the most important concepts and ideas he had used for decades to develop leaders around the world? When any of us choose to be leaders, what are we actually choosing to practise in our life?"

The page had four words on it: Reflect, Inquire, Pause and Act.

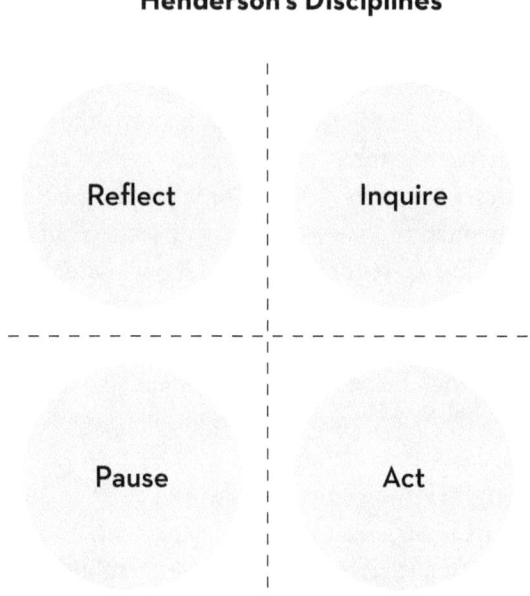

When It Is Time to Reflect

When I first saw Reflect as a core practice of leadership on Robert's notepad, I balked. To me the word had a nuance of passivity or softness, somehow. It was hard for me to imagine a situation on the farm I'd grown up on where my dad asked me to jump into a grain truck and I explained to him that "I can't right now because I'm reflecting." That would just not have gone well.

As it turns out, however, reflection isn't passive at all. When it is done properly, it's intensive and rigorous. It's about bringing as much information about a situation to the table as possible, and from a wide array of sources: past events, metrics, ratings, facts, perceptions, emotions, intuition. Information from the clear light of day, and from the shadows. Information we like the looks of, and that which takes courage to face. All of it.

When we have as much information as we can glean from a given situation, we comb through it—finding links, sorting into categories, making sense of what is in front of us. We come to coherence in the way we carry whatever *is*.

To perform this digging and organizing involves the recognition of patterns and connections. Reflection dares us to be thoughtful and discerning in our interpretation of all that we are exposed to. Through proper reflection, we come to a deeper understanding of what we are faced with, no matter how challenging it is. It's the grasping of what we know, the identification of what we don't and the gaining of insight, perspective and wisdom.

Much of a mentor's work is to create the space for reflection and to help someone else make sense of their experience. This involves taking an inventory of everything around a leader, and also within them. It involves crafting questions, requests and assignments for leaders to dig into. It requires using the way we conduct ourselves to create the psychological safety for people to say unpolished things and to learn from their experience.

There are times in our lives when the necessity of reflecting this way is obvious: when we choose where to live, who to partner with or which opportunities to undertake to change the nature of our work. But it is important that we recognize our chances to reflect in smaller and smaller realms as well: *What do I know about the person in front of me? What are themes that have come up in our conversations? What might they need from me?*

When It Is Time to Inquire

Great leaders ask well-crafted questions. They notice a change in your tone and ask a question about it. When they sense your discomfort, hear a whisper in the hallway or catch a glimpse of something in the parking lot, they ask a question about it. And they craft the kinds of questions that stop those around them in their tracks—questions that help a team, an organization, a community, even a country to stop, look around and re-find a better way forward. Harriet Beecher Stowe asked, "Is man ever a creature to be trusted with wholly irresponsible power?" Abraham Lincoln asked, "Do I not destroy my enemies when I make them my friends?" Martin Luther King Jr. referred to "life's most persistent and urgent question: 'What are you doing for others?'"

Valuable questions come from a place of curiosity and a desire to explore. They create a clean slate for others to populate with intel and insights. They surface what is not yet known or disclosed. The discipline of inquiry involves the careful tracking of the red-hot thread that weaves its way through the conversation. As we will explore in chapter 14, this is not something people are used to practising. We are conditioned to provide answers over crafting questions. Becoming the kind of mentor who can just as easily craft questions will take practice.

Mentors need to return again and again to what they are most curious about. They need to find out what their mentees are curious about. They need to start collecting great questions together and from each other. They need to be curious about the world together—and to draw questions from deep wells of intuition and instinct. They need to seek out new things to be curious about, taking field trips to experience things that interest them, the way Steve and Robert took a day to drive up to the Isle of Skye together to experience something they had read about in the newspaper. Mentors need to let go of being a source of answers and, instead, *wonder* with their mentees. They need to admit that so much of life and living is a mystery—and that our only relationship to a mystery is through our questions.

When It Is Time to Pause

Seeing Reflect on Robert's notepad made me anxious. But seeing Pause as one of the four practices of leadership sent me into a state approaching panic.

"Leaders aren't pausers," I said.

To me *pausing* sounded too much like *reflection*. With only four words in this framework, I was not prepared to carry them both.

Which is when Robert helped me understand that pausing and reflecting are complete opposites.

Reflection is about filling our mind with the focus of our reflection. Pausing is about *emptying* our mind. Pausing is the experience of deep rest and restoration; to pause properly is to replenish and recharge our resources. It's an act of appreciating our humanness and a recognition of the balance required to do our very best work—work the world needs from us.

The great benefit to a leader who can empty their mind is the choice of what goes back in when it's time to reflect, inquire or act. This discernment about which information is now important creates agility and resilience in the face of adversity and challenge.

In Roy Group's work, we notice that the most capable and sophisticated leaders have a steady relationship with pausing. It's in the relationship they have with free time, in the strategies they use to reground themselves in a difficult situation, in how they use their breath to reset between demanding conversations on the agenda. It's in their ability to switch off—and then to switch back on.

Mentors need to be an example of this relationship with pausing for the leaders they work with. They need to advocate for the dire necessity of pausing; without it we are less human, and that makes us a lesser leader. A mentor must help leaders experience pausing as a practice of leadership, not an escape from it. Mentors need to check in to ask how their mentees are pausing and how often. They need to challenge our culture's attitude that more is more, and that being busy is the way we excel. Mentors need to pause with and enjoy each other, and those they are working with.

Take pausing seriously as an integral component of your practice.

When It Is Time to Act

I was greatly relieved to see Act in the bottom right-hand corner of Robert's model. This is what leadership was all about to me (which is why I had so much to learn). In a moment that counts, this is what we see leaders do. Leaders say what needs to be said and do what needs to be done. They kick some ass. And they get up the next morning and do it again.

When Robert spoke of action, though, he was never talking about being busy. He wasn't talking about long lists of things that need to be done and checking them off from top to bottom. He was talking about right action: the right move at the right place at the right time. Right action is nothing more or less than what is required. It is the result of honed practice in the moments that count. It's masterful execution unhindered by doubt. It is the full, agile and balanced expression of our resolve. It's how leaders *actually* kick some ass.

Mentors need to create the space for leaders to find and prepare for right action. Mentors push us through feeling silly about dry runs, role-plays or dress rehearsals, and come through the other side with us to get our head in the game. Mentors need to help leaders get to a place of knowing how they will play the situation in front of them. They help mentees stay focused on their state of mind, the desired outcome and the strategy for getting there. They help mentees uncover risks that were just below the surface—and opportunities to accomplish more than we could have imagined.

One important nuance to note. The four words on Robert's page were separated by dotted lines. These represent the hesitation that comes when we don't know what it is time for. In the areas next to the dotted lines, leaders often become tempted into hybridizing the disciplines—doing more than one at a time. Robert explained that this was not ideal. Any moment provides the chance to dive deeply into *one* of the four. Proper practice means bringing the self-discipline to do just one at a time.

Becoming a mentor will involve

- beginning with the quiet question, "What is it time for?";
- practising these four disciplines alongside leaders;
- identifying opportunities for leaders to engage each discipline more fully; and
- enhancing the depth and quality with which leaders practise each discipline.

Henderson's Disciplines encapsulate the four practices we must embrace as leaders. If we are ever to become mentors to our next generation of leaders, we will have to help them practise, too.

REFLECTION

- What are your favourite ways to reflect, inquire, pause and take action?
- Think of a time recently when you have done these things in a disciplined way.

MEDITATION
Reign Over the Moments of Your Life

Reign over the moments of your life.
Bring gravity to the space you hold.
Like a mountain—solid and steady.
Allow others to count on you for this
and the awareness that comes
from being with you at the summit.

Reign over the moments of your life.
Send the clear message to the person you are with
that they are safe to surround you both
with anything and everything that is true for them.
And that you will focus on it all with them
until the way forward is clear enough to move.

Reign over the moments of your life.
Trust your instinct
to create just the right balance
of structure and of space
so that the single spark of imagination
becomes the raging fire.

Reign over the moments of your life.
Keep your careful promises.
Acquire high expectation of those next to you
to do the same and hold them to these standards.
Outdo your opponents in honour.

Reign over the moments of your life.
Be drawn to adversity.
Bring the light inside you to difficult circumstance.
Position yourself in realities
that are tough and worn down from friction.
And remind those with you that we are not built for easy.

Reign over the moments of your life.
Choose judiciously but do not judge
the paths you encounter.
Do not dare to feign humility.
Do not question what you could possibly do.
Ascend. Serve. Reign.

5

The Primacy of Conduct

I am the decisive element in the classroom.
It is my personal approach that creates the climate.
It is my daily mood that makes the weather.
As a teacher I possess tremendous power to make
a child's life miserable or joyous.

DR. HAIM G. GINOTT

UNDERSTAND THERE are some mixed messages in the chapters that brought us here.

I've asked you to not use the word *mentor* to describe yourself—yet am writing a book to help you earn the very word. Is this path of mentorship all about you, as we discussed in chapters 3 and 4, or about the next generation of leaders?

Paradoxically, the Athena Signature is both.

Being highly aware of yourself while keeping your attention completely focused on someone else is what mentorship is all about.

This Is Going to Change Everything

If you and I were in some strange situation where I had the chance to share only a single conviction with you—a principle that underlines everything this journey is about—this would be it:

The way you choose to conduct yourself creates an atmosphere inside others.

Let's start with *conduct*. It's an old-fashioned word conveying a nuance of things being done properly or well. We hear the word *misconduct* more nowadays, especially in the news.

Your conduct is where everything that's going on inside you meets the rest of the world. It is the envelope and the user interface. It's what you say, how you move, the expression you wear, the tone of your voice. Your conduct is the last thing you hold in your control in that final moment when you have 100 percent choice, 100 percent autonomy, in any given situation. Once you've made that choice and conducted yourself a certain way, it's not in your control anymore. Choose unconsciously and you open the door to any number of complications and unintended consequences.

But choose a way of conducting yourself that you've worked on consciously and discerningly, and it can provide you with the remarkable ability to steer any story to where it needs to go.

Atmosphere, on the other hand, I use because we *can't* control it. When we step outside our home in the morning, we sense the temperature of the air around us on our skin, the day's humidity, the movement of nearby leaves... but we can't shape it or change it. It just is. And everyone we meet is the same inside: a neurochemical soup that changes and evolves as they move through their day.

This, then, is the combination: your conduct and their atmosphere. One gives us a choice, and the other doesn't—but the choices I make from moment to moment shape how someone else experiences themselves. This represents an influence that most of us don't even know we have.

And there's another important nuance to the relationship between conduct and atmosphere.

Most of the time, that other person's brain can't just let an atmosphere be something they *sense*. Their brain—evolved across millennia for survival—is programmed to take that sensation inside and make it mean something. The neocortex is relentless in its creation of meaning, its drive to convert sense data into a story.

Imagine this scene:

You're at a reception, about to interact with someone you've been wanting to meet for some time. If you make a good first impression it might lead to some opportunities. More than that, you think highly of this person and what they've accomplished. So you're strongly motivated to show up well.

You engage, and to your delight this person engages back. It's as if they've been wanting to meet you, too! They then ask questions that provide you with an opening to explain what you and your team do. It's the opportunity you've been waiting for, so you begin to set the table in a compelling way, with all the favourite points that you know connect with people.

You're just entering the most impactful part of your description—that phrase you know this person will take away, consider and probably pass on to someone else—when something changes. You notice they've spotted someone they need to talk to over your shoulder. There's a tremor in the force. All is not as right as it was just moments ago.

You persevere with your explanation. But this person seems worried they might miss their chance to connect with that person behind you. Your attention starts to splinter. It feels like you're treading water, trying even harder now to say things in an interesting way.

The atmosphere inside you shifts from being something that just *is* to a collection of insidious little conclusions. And the most well-travelled neural pathways to fire are the ones that make this situation mean something about yourself.

I am not in this person's league.
I am not articulate.
I am not interesting.
I am wasting their time.
I am not smart.
I am not enough.
I am not important.

Maybe you doubted yourself before the interaction. You saw that person as an authority and felt the dizzying influence of celebrity, even a bit of a crush. This atmosphere was quickly converted to meaning and then transformed into an arbitrary and limiting set of beliefs about yourself.

With this clarified awareness of how conduct creates an atmosphere inside other people, you're going to start seeing this powerful cause-and-effect relationship in every corner of your existence. At work, at home, in the community. One person conducts themselves a certain way, and it shapes what others believe about themselves in that moment.

With all the interactions we engage in every day, I wonder, *what atmospheres are we leaving behind? And what are people making that mean about themselves?*

I realize there's some weight to this. I'm asking you to take full responsibility for your conduct. This will be in addition to everything you're already responsible for, which I know is considerable. I apologize. But this is the moment when there is no going back; that is behind us now. We have to keep moving forward.

It takes a substantial amount of practice to show up for people in some signature way that brings out the best in them. It starts with knowing that this dynamic happens in the first place. It takes being lit with energy and focus from the inside. It takes attention and a desire to understand where another person is coming from. It takes generosity of spirit, compassion and composure, a sense of humour and a sense of honour. It requires that you see every opportunity to connect as a chance to push yourself, the way an athlete or an artist does, to become more agile and more able to show up the way people need you to.

It takes presence—occupying the ground in a way that signals to someone that they are important to you, that you know what they're tackling is important to them. Presence is the ability to be in the here and now with someone. It is the gift of being grounded, steady and solid for someone. It is the embodiment of patience, belief and non-judgment—the taking command of your conduct, and making the way you show up a lifeline to the person in front of you.

The Athena Signature takes practice.

The way you choose
to conduct yourself
creates an atmosphere
inside others.

The exciting part of this conviction is that we can, in fact, learn how to use the way we show up as a force for good. You can choose the way you conduct yourself to create a positive atmosphere in others, which gets translated into a positive set of conclusions.

How might we conduct ourselves in a way that leaves a list like this inside another person?

I am fun to be with.
It is safe for me to be honest.
I'm intelligent and articulate.
I am capable.
I am calm.
I'm clear about what needs to be done.
I have a gift that the world needs.
I am a leader of important endeavours.
I am not alone.

Quiet champions make a silent choice to shape the state they wish to leave others in. Underneath the transcript of whatever is being said lies this difference, this fork in the path, which leads to two different kinds of stories unfolding next. The first list, from the reception scenario, unfolds in the form of a mediocre story—the kind of story that people "get through" but don't thrive in. There's just something getting in the way of performing, learning and engaging deeply. The last thing we need.

What are the kinds of stories that unfold from the second list? What actions do people find themselves taking if *these* are their beliefs about themselves? What kinds of stories emerge when people on your team and in your community show up this way for each other? Where they engage, notice and learn from every moment, together? Where they believe in themselves and each other? Where they perform their hearts out because there's nothing getting in the way?

It all starts with the way you choose to conduct yourself.

A Sense of Sovereignty

Sovereignty is a loaded word. It's also deeply relevant to what we're wrapping our minds around here.

I once sat down with a special mentor of mine named Tim Gallwey. Tim's groundbreaking book, *The Inner Game of Tennis*, was published in 1974, kick-starting much of what we know today as "the coaching approach." The book broke new ground by suggesting that the biggest obstacles to improvement are internal: negative self-talk, doubt and limiting beliefs. Concepts we're still reading a lot about today.

I was given a copy of *The Inner Game of Tennis* as a young CEO, just 27. A decade later, a thoughtful acquaintance introduced me to Tim, and one of our first private discussions was about my conviction that personal conduct shapes the atmosphere in others. Tim was someone who I'd seen conduct himself in an exquisite way with people, a way that invited the very best from those around him.

After what felt like a lot of effort to explain myself, he asked me point-blank if I felt "sovereign."

Intuitively, I felt the weight of this word without really understanding all the implications. I *did* have a sense that I was, in fact, sovereign... somehow.

"Then what are you sovereign over?" Tim asked.

I paused. To be *sovereign* literally means *to reign over*. Now the question had a very uncomfortable edge, with no clear answers.

I struggled. His question felt like a trap.

He tried again. "Do you reign over your family?"

"No." He obviously had never met my children.

"Do you reign over your marriage?"

"Not at all."

"Do you reign over the team you lead?"

"No." Maybe I wasn't sovereign, after all.

"Do you reign over the company that you yourself own?"

I wanted to say yes. "No."

"This is the problem," he said. "You sense you're sovereign, but you can't tell me what it is that you are sovereign over."

I agreed with him. This was a dilemma.

He let that disconnect dangle in the room, like a sparking wire hanging from the ceiling, for just long enough that I found myself hoping we could move on to another topic.

At last he spoke. "Perhaps what we reign over are the moments of our life."

What a way to understand the way we choose to conduct ourselves: as sovereignty over the moments of our life. Exciting things enter the court in front of us, and each of us has a choice about how we reign over that moment. Challenging things enter, too, and we have a choice how we reign over that. And *any* moment.

There we are, asked to be discerning and thoughtful and wise—to be quietly sovereign in the way we conduct ourselves—the way Athena was.

What We Leave Behind

In listening to would-be mentors behind closed doors for three decades now, I'm interested in how often the conversation eventually comes around to focus on a person's legacy. *What is it that they're building? What do they want to pass forward to the next generation?* Underneath this wondering is the desire to leave a legacy that reflects a remarkable life lived.

Give people a chance to talk about what they want to leave behind, and you're tapping into who they are. You're unlocking what's possible just by encouraging them to give voice to what they would most like to accomplish. Quite often, this invitation makes people want to swing for the fences. Dreaming big feels good.

The longer I do this work, though, the more I find myself paying attention to smaller legacies. What is it that's left behind after a two-minute, twenty-minute or two-hour connection with you? My hunch is that if we pay attention to these tiny legacies, over and over—and to what we leave people believing about themselves—the big, audacious legacies will unfold the way they need to on their own.

I've met a number of people across my lifespan who carry the Athena Signature in their conduct. There's something about the way they interface with the world around them that reflects a honed practice of using their conduct as a catalyst in any situation they might encounter. Many of them were people I didn't know well; perhaps I met them in a social setting or crossed paths at a public event. They weren't a mentor to me, as such, but I recognized something I was fascinated with nonetheless. And I know that many others refer to these folks as mentors.

Dr. Tony Fields is one of these unique individuals. Now professor emeritus of the Department of Oncology at the University of Alberta, Fields was born and raised in Barbados. He moved to Canada in the 1960s and began a career of personal and professional excellence. By all accounts, Fields is an incredible physician and leader. When the topic of mentorship comes up, highly regarded doctors across the country and around the world talk about the way Fields conducts himself. One mentee described it this way: "Tony has a way of calming patients when he walks in the room. It's not something you can teach, but it is something you can model."

I noticed this immediately. His presence drew my attention almost exclusively over several hours of a robust day-long workshop, sitting in a circle with twenty-three other volunteers for a college mentor corps. I was struck by the kindness with which he listened to what other people had to say, and his humble way of being.

His attention was wholly set on the people in front of him. His careful and loving oversight came with no pressure on the people speaking to hurry up. He savoured the insights of others. As the facilitator, I found myself experiencing his quiet but total appreciation for the gathering I was convening. It was as if this man I had just met over coffee earlier that day was now proud of me, invested in me and present in the here and now for me.

He was *only* in the here, and *only* in the now. It was as if everything happening within this man was so clear and at peace that he had the ability to attune and create the space in front of him for what needed to happen. Through his exquisite way of showing up, he created a sense of safety, belonging and community. He created a shared awareness for all of us that we were worthy of each other's respect.

When the topic of conduct came up, Fields shared an example of something he'd been noticing for years. He presented a scenario that represents one of the most difficult things an oncologist has to do:

deliver troubling news to a patient and their family. Fields noticed that many of his interns would instinctively stand near the door in these situations. Some would even keep their hand on the doorknob. Fields didn't judge this. He suspected this behaviour came from an understandable place: that the intern believed their job was to deliver the information as clearly as possible, and then respectfully leave the patient with their loved ones to absorb the blow and begin to process their emotions.

Of course, breaking bad news while edging towards the exit isn't the right move. Whenever Fields was in the room and saw this about to happen, he would quietly remove the intern's hand from the door handle and steer them gently to go and sit with the family before they started their discussion. Fields is an expert in the medical space, so he understands the *what*: the science, the research and the treatment processes his interns are about to explain. But as a practitioner and mentor, he also understands the importance of the *how*.

The Way Mentors Conduct Themselves

The best way I can describe the Athena Signature is as a paradoxically universal yet deeply personal sweet spot of settings on the soundboard of the way we conduct ourselves. It somehow sends a signal that we know who we are in the world and have the appetite to help others be the same way. The Athena Signature lets people know that, as best we can, we will be a safe harbour from the tempest. This approach signals that we are open, accessible and prepared to invest all of who we are. It communicates that we will, at every turn, commit to replacing judgment with curiosity and compassion. It promises patience, understanding and genuine interest.

At its core, the Athena Signature is kind, capable, loving and wise.

The Athena Signature creates a space of *here* that others can return to again and again—in triumph, in failure, in doubt and in struggle. It invites the best of someone to come out and join this challenging, exciting, sometimes deeply painful dance called life. It invites our finest self to be seen and sensed and counted on.

It whispers that *I have all the time in the world for you*—which of course is never true.

My relationship with mentors from a young age has been the single most transformational force in my evolution. It wasn't perfect. In fact, it bore all kinds of human imperfections. But as a collective investment by other people in developing my finest self, mentorship has changed the trajectory of my life. It has invited me to be fully who I am. It has provided me with the courage to be in over my head. I feel very fortunate to be able to write all of that—and sad to think there are many people who have never experienced this presence in their life. (Yet.)

The sheer number of hours I've spent with quiet champions like Tony Fields over the past thirty years has given me insights into both the potential of a world served by mentorship, and what gets in the way of mentorship happening. Closely observing team dynamics like this has given me the chance to recognize some patterns in the way the most impactful mentors conduct themselves. Of course, each one of them has their own style, but underneath each unique way there is the crux of the Athena Signature: high self-awareness paired with a disciplined focus on the emergent experience of others. As part of this signature, six attributes of their conduct show themselves over and over again.

1. Mentors are solid and steady.

My mentors have a way of minimizing drama and distraction even when it surrounds a situation. They have a way of creating safety for me to disclose what's really going on. Bad news or complications don't rock them; this just increases their level of focus. I am free to be rocked by what I face, but my mentor's belief in me is not diminished. I am free to experience any emotion I need to. A mentor's steadiness creates the space for it all to come out.

When I'm with them, they make me feel as though there's nothing else going on in the world except this conversation. They are quietly but noticeably fascinated with what I am facing. The conversation is centred on my experience more than theirs—even though I know their experience is considerable, present and available. I feel that what I am leading is important, and that I'm able to assess the challenges in front of me with all the relevant information on the table—even in the face of fear. And they still want to know more, pointing my attention here and there to dig deeper into what is really going on.

The way my mentors conduct themselves invites my *awareness*.

2. Mentors have an unflinching desire for honesty.

My mentors share a way of providing and encouraging honesty. They want to know what's really going on. They want to know what's difficult, not just what's working well. They can sense if I'm hiding the rough edges of a situation, or being overly diplomatic in my assessment.

I know they expect honesty from me, and they give me no reason not to provide it. They remind me that I'm behind closed doors and that our conversation is confidential—and that unless I get honest with myself, nothing's going to change.

They help me understand what's really at play. If their observations are deeply uncomfortable, it's because they're true. And it's time to get real.

The way my mentors conduct themselves invites my *focus*.

3. Mentors provide a balance of structure and space.

My mentors consistently find a way to get this balance right. They have a favourite place to meet up with me. When time allows or the situation requires, they deploy an interesting tactic or bring out a model to guide our conversation—something they've read that's worth sharing, something or someone they've heard about. They are keen for me to set up my next time with them. Which never ceases meaning the world to me—that they want to continue our conversations.

They bring their favourite methods for thinking things through and moving forward. They provide a powerful *how* so that I can conceptualize the *what*. They bring the relevant crucibles to hold all of the unique content I need to create—or destroy. This gives me the confidence to tackle any situation I need to in a way I couldn't have imagined on my own.

They bring a deftness to their shifting of gears in the conversation. They show up in a way that I want to emulate for others. There is rigor, but there is also room. Most of all, there's a reverence for what I need to bring into being.

The way my mentors conduct themselves invites my *creativity*.

4. Mentors hold me in high regard, and to high standards.

My mentors have taken the time to get to know me and where I come from. They appreciate my strengths and help me acknowledge my weaknesses. They provide clear examples of when I've been at my best. They help me identify the conditions I thrive in, and remind me to do this as often as they need to. They help me understand my unique gifts and how to use them. They help me stay true.

They know who I am, and can remind me of that with a momentary look up from their notes. They expect *special* from me. They expect discretionary effort—and they know I will bring it. In situations where tough calls are required, they ultimately trust my best judgment, even if they have to remind me to trust it, too. They remind me to only make promises I can keep. And that what I am about to go and do *counts*.

The way my mentors conduct themselves invites my work to come from a deep source of *integrity*.

5. Mentors have ways of communicating unconditional twists of joy.

My mentors enjoy me, and their time with me. They've straight-up told me this, even though they didn't need to. I could tell they did. They send me signals through the noise: a nod, a timely smile, a discreet wink, a confirming hand on the shoulder. These little moments of connection send a message straight to my heart: "Here we are, together at another important juncture in life. Imagine that."

These moments of connection are achievement-agnostic—they aren't just shared when I'm winning. They're on tap, a constant, through thick and thin, humbly offered in my triumphs and generously offered in my train wrecks. It is in those hardest times that

The Athena Signature creates a space of here that others can always return to—
in triumph, in failure, in doubt and in struggle.

signals like this mean even more, conveying an understanding of the pain alongside a regret that they couldn't spare me from it. Their own scars are undeniable evidence that I can tap into whatever I need to keep going. Like they did when they had to.

The way my mentors conduct themselves invites my *perseverance*.

6. Mentors do not judge.

My mentors know I'm learning from my experience and help to deepen that learning. They act like they have all the time in the world for me, even though they lead very demanding lives. They challenge my thinking, not because it's faulty but because it's not yet fully formed.

They allow me to say unpolished things, unpleasant things, even things I don't even really believe, but I have to say them out loud to get past them.

They ask me questions that make me dig. They want to find out more. They help me organize what we find. And they affirm my choices that do something valuable and needed in the world. They trust that I'm doing what I do for some wonderful reason. They remind me to trust my swing.

The way my mentors conduct themselves invites my *service* to the world.

These six qualities—*awareness, focus, creativity, integrity, perseverance* and *service*—are what the next generation of leaders is going to need to navigate the choppy waters ahead. So we are going to need to be examples of those qualities. And we also are going to need to conduct ourselves in a way that brings out these qualities in *them*. A serious responsibility to be sure.

One you've spent your whole life preparing for.

TACTIC Ascending to the LOFT

Because conduct plays such a strong role in how we influence other people and situations, it's important to have a practical tool that we can use to raise our game just before an important interaction.

I often use the idea of ascending to the LOFT—showing up for someone else Lit, Open, Focused and Transparent—in my conduct.

This allows me to quickly assess my readiness to engage properly and make any needed adjustments.

As I ready and steady myself to engage, I rate each of my LOFT attributes on a scale of 1 to 10:

1. **How Lit am I on the inside?**
   Have I protected my energy reserves in advance of this interaction? How noticeable will my energy be to the person or group I'm about to interact with? How strongly is the light inside me burning? How ready am I to experience and add to the light of others?

2. **How Open am I prepared to be?**
   How curious am I about what other people have to contribute to these discussions? How much might I be able to find out about these other people? How open am I to the idea that I may be missing some important perspectives? How forgiving am I prepared to be if I experience any rough edges in the way others communicate?

3. **How Focused am I prepared to be?**
   How ready am I to pay full attention? How clear am I about any intentions I'm bringing to this conversation? How proactive have I been to remove any potential distractions? How strong is my belief that my focus is a gift to others?

4. **How Transparent am I prepared to be?**
   How ready am I to describe my current state? How prepared am I to share important information? How keen am I to notice the patterns in and under this conversation? How honest am I prepared to be about what I notice?

Remember: It's about self-awareness.

If I score a quality at 8, what is getting in the way of it being a 10? Address that, and your behaviour changes.

REFLECTION

- Who is someone in the story of your life who has earned the word *mentor*?
- What was it about their conduct that earned them the word?

MEDITATION
Stay True

Stay true.
Honour the trust others have placed in you
by being trustworthy,
moment after moment, again and again.
Kind and candid with yourself
about what is integrating and disintegrating.

Stay true.
Noticing what you notice
about the pattern of light and shadows
within you and around you.
Tending with care to bring more and more light
to learn from missteps.

Stay true.
Your craft speaks for itself.
We see what you have created and what you share
in every cell of your being.
It has connected you to others
who know you and all you stand for.

Stay true.
Be generous with your spending of time.
What reaps a currency of one kind—lays fire to another.
And a good life needs them all.
Even though we are quiet—it is crystal clear to us
what being honourable is worth to you.

Stay true.
Take responsibility for the power you have.
Wield it honestly without deception or pretense.
Place it carefully and selflessly to move stories forward,
making a sacred promise to yourself
to do no harm.

Stay true.
Notice what is true.
Acknowledge what is true.
Forgive what is true.
Choose to propel yourself towards what is true.
And stay the course.

6

Staying Clear of Pitfalls

Good moral character is not something that we can achieve on our own. We need a culture that supports the conditions under which self-love and friendship flourish.
ARISTOTLE

THE DEPTHS BENEATH human relationships never cease to amaze me.

Any human relationship, even one that looks simple on the surface, is fraught with complexities and unseen patterns below the surface. These depths, in the vast majority of cases, need not be frightening as much as interesting. The one-of-a-kind path that each person has travelled creates a totally unique pattern of light and shadow within them. And then our paths collide for an even more one-of-a-kind intersection.

In these interactions we simultaneously evolve into something we have never been before, and devolve into past patterns we may not even be aware of in the moment. Each relationship changes us and brings new aspects to the surface. The relationships between us integrate and disintegrate—at different rates, through different experiences, in different contexts. They are created, they evolve, they become something distinct, and sometimes they come to an end.

The relationship between mentor and mentee is no different. It can be a strong connection over a lifetime, but it also may rupture and come to an end due to something that one or both parties have contributed to. It represents a power dynamic that invites mentors to be as careful, thoughtful and wise as they can be. In all cases, it will change along the way—something to be conscious of and open to. Like any relationship, it needs to evolve and find its new edges.

Whenever we choose to invest our time, resources and focus into a relationship, somewhere underneath it is the return on our investment that we would like to see. This is where mentors need to keep themselves (and each other) very much in check. There are key motivations of fulfillment, connection and enjoyment that will deepen trust, capacity and belonging—but there is also a range of motivations that have the potential to do harm.

Like in any relationship, these alternative motivations create risks that need to be managed, mitigated or eliminated. As a mentor, you are primarily responsible for staying aware of these potential pitfalls. Awareness going into a mentor relationship allows you to be *canny*—a wonderful Scottish word for being wide awake and ready to respond to weak signals early—and able to navigate through important territory in a way that reduces risk and maximizes positive impact. By bringing this acute awareness, we reduce damage to the relationship and those in it, now and into the future.

The Pitfalls of Status, Profile and Profit

A few decades ago, I took part in a group exercise designed to make participants aware of our keen—and largely unconscious—perception of status. At the end of a very demanding day, all of us but five participants were asked to take a card from a deck of playing cards and keep it to ourselves. We were then requested to attend a private reception before dinner that evening, and to arrive at the event acting congruent with our "rank" as determined by the card we had chosen.

The five individuals who hadn't selected a card were observers and given a secret assignment that the rest of us weren't privy to.

We arrived at the reception, finding all kinds of subtle and creative ways to demonstrate our station in relation to the others. Half an hour in, the observers were asked to organize everyone in the room from lowest to highest based on how they had conducted themselves at the party.

I was pretty sure the observers would get general groupings right. The face cards and aces had acted suitably regal. The folks with anything less than a four were pretty easy to spot. Everyone in between would be a guess.

Instead the five observers grouped people up with near-perfect accuracy. A few sevens ended up in the line above the eights, but otherwise the observers' diagnosis of the status range was flawless.

Status is obviously something we're attuned to pick up cues for. The game of status is one we play with each other all the time. People are always positioning and playing politics. It is part of our nature. Which means it's a substantial request when I ask mentors to stop and set this game aside.

I have seen the appetite for status tarnish more mentor relationships than I can count. It starts quite innocently: A mentor gives in to their desire to feel important, recognized and somehow superior. It changes the dynamic—a little at first, but over time creating a status gradient that will bring the relationship to its end.

For some mentors, an appetite for status can create a habit of attaching their name to successes with their mentees. I've seen mentorship become a way insecure adults address a bottomless appetite for recognition and praise, shaping their own reputations and building their profile through association with successful individuals. This isn't a problem in itself... unless those ventures start to fail. Then the relationships that provided the status boost to the mentor become a *risk* to their status, and they must distance themselves to protect what is most important: themselves.

There's also risk for these mentors at the other end of the spectrum—if the venture becomes too successful, and the protégé begins to achieve more than their mentor has. If a mentor's identity is tied too tightly to being the most important character in the relationship, the mentee can never move beyond that. The mentor starts either subtly manoeuvring to remain an impressive "ace," or unconsciously manipulating things to keep their mentee a "seven." Growth is stymied. Now there are strings attached. An unconscious message is sent: *You can be a big deal, just not a bigger deal than me.* Not a dynamic Athena would tolerate.

Another motivation that mentors must be careful with is profit—that is, when a relationship may involve a financial return. There are many arrangements where a mentor may also be a supervisor with reward incentives tied to the performance of one's team, or a financial investor in a venture being led by a mentee. Once again, it is important for any mentor to keep such motivations in check.

If you find yourself in a mentor relationship where you're receiving a financial return of any kind, a key question to ask yourself is this: *Is my desire for personal gain greater than my motivation to see this mentee grow, learn and become their finest self?* If it is, there's a conflict of interest that must be addressed, talked about and brought back into balance.

The great benefit of not having this conflict of interest is that the mentee has no reason to question why you're in their corner. Our world doesn't need mentors who attach their wagons only to winning horses. Nor do we need mentors who conveniently step out of situations when conditions start to become challenging. We need mentors who quietly step into play when conditions are dire and they are needed the most. We need mentors who sense the potential in people and stick with them through thick and thin.

The Pitfall of Unclear Boundaries

The motto of the Law Society of Scotland is *Humani nihil alienum*, taken from the full quote of Roman playwright and poet Terence: "*Homo sum; humani nil a me alienum puto.*" In full it means, "I am a human being. Nothing that is human is alien to me."

In writing this section, this expression of deep and transformational compassion has come to mind over and over again. This idea doesn't mean that anything any human ever does is right, or even

We need mentors who quietly step into play when conditions are dire and they are needed the most.

acceptable. It doesn't mean we condone dynamics that we know cause harm, or that there are no consequences for one's actions. It means we are invited to be curious and as non-judgmental as possible, for as long as possible, until the greatest possible understanding is achieved.

Over the past few decades, some patterns have emerged in my conversations with leaders about mentorship. Many of these patterns are positive and constitute the chapters of this book. One, however, has troubled me. It contradicts my deep belief that mentorship always represents a force for good. It is a pattern that I believe has been shaped by centuries of gender roles, power dynamics, societal norms and taboos. And it causes boatloads of damage and pain.

The pattern occurs when older men (primarily) are paired with younger women (primarily) in some form of mentorship arrangement. (I am certain the specifics of this will vary in every combination possible.) The setting might be a college, workplace, industry group or community program. Perhaps the mentor is a teacher, coach or volunteer who is deemed by society as being trustworthy and put forward into a mentorship role. The mentor-mentee relationship takes shape. Then comes the pitfall: After a length of time and to varying degrees of surprise or mutuality, the mentor confesses that he is having deeper feelings of attraction to his mentee.

(As much as this represents the crossing of a clear line to me—the very real leveraging of a power differential—I want to set judgment aside and appreciate that there is a wide range of other situations where this may happen.)

The mentees' responses to this confession can include shock, rejection, resistance, polite sidestepping, confusion and in some cases reciprocation (with varying degrees of reluctance). There is often damage—to reputations, to the relationship, to adjacent relationships—but most notably to the mentee's ability to trust mentorships again, feeling that there will always be this sexual subtext present.

In the surprisingly common stories shared with me, the emergent desire for a physically intimate relationship came from three categories. In examples at the ugliest end of the spectrum, mentorship was a guise from the very beginning. All contact was an effort to groom someone for a sexual relationship with very little regard for the person's development or well-being. In the last few years, these discussions have taken place surrounded by the #MeToo movement, which I believe has brought more of these stories into the light of day and the conversations we're having. It is predatory behaviour and a clear abuse of power, and I believe it needs to be met with harsh consequences.

At the other end of the spectrum, I've heard stories of genuine and mutual love between people who just happened to meet each other in the context of mentorship. In whatever form this takes in the long term, there still may be consequences. But I cannot judge love—or the choices people make when they find it.

In between these two extremes lie the majority of examples I hear about: A mentor experiences an attraction that is clearly outside the bounds of mentorship and chooses to act on it, without understanding where the desire is coming from.

This is where mentors have an opportunity to do the right thing and speak to someone outside the situation about it—before they approach their mentee. The feelings are what they are. Acting on them in haste, though, is irresponsible. Some proper reflection is required here, perhaps supported by a professional, or at least a good friend. Mentors need to confide in each other about these kinds of motivations and where they are actually coming from.

Here are two questions mentors can ask each other to assist:

1. Is what you are feeling actually attraction to a person, or to an idea that this person represents—a new start, a clean slate, a reclaimed youth, being impressive to someone, or the chance to somehow be less flawed than you are with the people in your long-term relationships?
2. Could you be breaking trust or causing harm to this person if you express these feelings?

With proper reflection, inquiry and pause, right action becomes clear. Right action may involve bringing an end to the relationship for the good of all involved. Or it might mean a renewed commitment to the mentorship relationship, unhindered by complication.

But any consciously chosen way forward is an opportunity for mentors to act honourably.

The mentorship dynamic is at its healthiest when what is motivating it is true and uncompromised: the selfless fulfillment that comes from accompanying someone as they take steps down the long, hard road of re-finding their finest self in this life.

That sounds simple, but it isn't. Finding our own finest self from moment to moment is hard enough, let alone assisting someone else along. But this is the gig. Each of us, a work in progress, putting in the time and effort to bring each other along.

The wise among you will know that we never get there—to our finest self, that is. But each reflection makes us capable of even richer perspective. Each question we ask allows us to find out a little bit more. Each pause we take allows for a new and more formidable beginning. Each accomplishment makes us capable of the next, even greater achievement. There is no end to this journey, so we must focus on the way we make it.

Will you make your journey about curiosity, or will you hang on to the idea of all-knowingness? Will you make your journey with a high degree of personal responsibility, or will you permit your integrity to wobble? Are you prepared to occupy the ground of mentorship honourably, even if that requires sacrifice, foresight and sometimes painful self-discovery?

Beneath all of the potential pitfalls within mentorship is the question of what motivates us: our awareness of these motivations, our compassion in understanding where they come from and our accountability for the actions we take to move forward.

Staying conscious of our motivations as mentors is a challenge—and an imperative. It requires that we look into the shadows of our own psyches to see glimpses of where these forces come from. And then going deeper to understand the often painful roots of their influence over our actions. Before you damage a working relationship by acting on your impulses, have a look at this list of examples. These are some deep currents that might shape our tendencies in a mentor relationship:

- The shame of a fall from status in our community has made us relentlessly hungry to gain a national profile. We sacrifice deeper long-term relationships for being impressive to a rolling list of new and well-connected acquaintances.
- The embarrassment of being called weak drives us to be heavy-handed in what we say to others. We begin to pride ourselves on how critical we can be, when really our quick bluntness protects us from ever showing vulnerability.
- A pattern of proving ourselves to others has created an addiction to work. We drive ourselves to depletion and judge others who we deem are not as hard-working as we are.
- That all-too-human feeling that we don't belong tempts us to please others at all costs to win them over. Or we go the other way, finding every opportunity to demonstrate our superiority.
- Being abandoned or rejected in the past has us angling to manipulate a deeper sense of intimacy and accumulate power over someone in the present.

Setting self-judgment aside does not mean zero accountability.

———————————

Being conscious of where our appetites are coming from is an uncomfortable and often tender effort. But these unconscious appetites aren't good or bad. They just are. What we would normally do as soon as we become aware of them is to judge them—and to judge ourselves. I suggest we take the energy that we would otherwise beat ourselves up with and channel it into contemplation and compassion. Compassion for self, understanding that any human experience is one that puts a dent or two (or forty-seven) in us, finding ways to forgive ourselves for being human—this is a much better way to go. It makes us more capable of helping others do the same, with empathy and understanding, and without judgment.

Setting self-judgment aside does not mean zero accountability. Just because I understand where the impetus for a certain behaviour is coming from doesn't mean I am justified to take actions that will hurt another person. For so many reasons outlined in this book—that this is about who you are, about being a person of practice, about being an example, about shaping someone else to be who they are capable of becoming—you are *required* to conduct yourself honourably.

When we are tempted by motivations like profile, profit and power for power's sake, we unintentionally introduce the possibility of damage. If we proceed unchecked and begin to take subconscious steps towards reaping these tempting extras, we compromise something otherwise pure. When we give in to desires for other rewards, we introduce unnecessary risk.

Of course there are stories of the reverse scenario—when a mentee confesses having feelings that fall outside the bounds of mentorship. In these cases, right action seems much clearer, precisely because of the power dynamic that exists. A mentor can be kind and understanding with this awareness, feeling deeply for a young person taking the risk to confess these feelings and steering things carefully and honourably to a place that does the least long-term harm. When we fail to take right action in these scenarios, people get hurt.

Helping Mentees Learn from Their Experience (with You)

A large part of our responsibility as mentors is to help our mentees learn from their experience. That includes—and perhaps begins with—learning from their experience with *you*, which provides the chance for mentees to attain, step by step, a set of attributes that will invite their future mentors to step up for them. Most of these attributes come down to a set of fundamentally good manners that nurture the relationship and make it valuable, reciprocal and respectful for both parties:

- Being conscientious about setting up times to connect.
- Consistently showing up on time.
- Showing up with real topics to address, along with important questions and insights.
- Showing up with energy, attention and enthusiasm, even when the topics are tough and the challenges steep.
- Checking in with mentors even when there isn't a short-term need from them.
- Bringing a genuine interest to what a mentor has to say, even if one disagrees.
- Admitting failure and dropping one's guard to display vulnerability.
- Showing appreciation and acknowledging the value of what is being offered by the mentor.

One of the things we can do for our mentees is help them cultivate these attributes so that over the course of their life, they become aware and capable of what it means to tend to a network of supportive and valuable relationships. Every misstep becomes an opportunity to help them be a better mentee and a better leader. Our honesty, transparency and kindness—and minimal judgment about any gaps in their good manners—can provide them with some valuable intelligence and inform modifications to the way they steward this and future relationships.

One way we can do this is by ritualizing a regular feedback conversation—like the one we will explore in chapter 14—that is focused on the mentor-mentee relationship, and use it to contract and re-contract going forward. Rather than waiting for a pattern to fester into an issue, we keep the slate clean at regular intervals by noticing and tabling the patterns we are conscious of and what we expect would make them more rewarding for us. A mentor can make this a standard practice—taking some time to step back from the content of discussions at regular intervals and discuss the container, something we are both responsible for making stronger and stronger.

TACTIC **Checking Motivation**

Draw a small circle on a page.

Inside that circle, write these words:

Their finest self.

Their finest contribution.

Add any other motivations (for example: friendship, profile, admiration) that are propelling your own actions in this relationship and position them outside the circle: Strong motivations belong close to the circle, and weak ones farther away.

Ask yourself:

- Which of these motivations are acceptable?
- Are there risks associated with them?
- How will I mitigate these risks?
- Are there motivations that seem particularly risky?
- Who can I speak to about these motivations? By when?

REFLECTION

- What is something that motivates you that you wish didn't?
- Are there ways you might approach a situation differently from how you have been?

MEDITATION
Be Exquisite in Your Execution

Be exquisite in your execution.
Drawing the attention of those who witness it.
Striking, explosive and impeccable.
Every moment seized.
Every resource available to you.
Woven into the focus of the flow.

Be exquisite in your execution.
Quietly and calmly
stacking each moment onto the next,
with intention.
And carefully holding
all that is at stake.

Be exquisite in your execution.
Transfix us by every move you make.
Make us want to soak it into who we are,
exchanging our very breath to imagine

how sweet the sensation
of being you must be.

Be exquisite in your execution.
So that we start to mouth the way you say it,
and engage the way we see you immerse.
What we see in you
is now a glimpse of our potential within
yearning to be expressed.

Be exquisite in your execution.
Share something worth sharing
down through time.
Live on through centuries
in the actions of those
who emulate those who emulate you.

Be exquisite in your execution.
A signature presence.
A signal through the noise.
A harbour from the storm.
Magician, lover, warrior and sovereign.
Be each and all of these things.

7

The Power of Example

Example is leadership.
ALBERT SCHWEITZER

WHEN PEOPLE tell stories about their mentors, it's very common to hear the theme, "All I have to do is watch the way this person does it, and I start doing it that way." It doesn't matter what the "it" is: a slapshot, a soliloquy, a brush stroke. The way a person works a room or negotiates a tricky situation at the board table. We learn and develop by watching and listening and noticing.

We especially notice when something is being done *well*. It's somehow wrapped in a different light that attracts our attention. It draws us in and whispers, "Could you ever do this that way?"

Our brains love to pay attention to a wide feed of sensory inputs. Yet we're also wired to narrow focus when something signals us as particularly relevant. This is what happens when we notice *flow*: we stop, and notice. Think how the gymnasium goes quiet when a gymnast is in top form. Or when Beyoncé sings a line that's meant just for you. You can't stop watching or listening. There's just nothing else going on in the world.

We're wired to stop and notice someone who's so deeply into their experience that they don't even see us. They're in flow—that state of total presence. Think of listening in on some imaginary scenario unfolding in your children's playhouse; you hang on every little share. We're wired to sense when someone is sharing their unique and signature gift with the world. Think of Barack Obama mid-speech, when he really gets rolling, or the way we lean forward on the couch when our favourite team ignites an epic comeback.

We're wired to notice the exquisite ease that comes with talent, years of practice and a moment that counts. Think of how fast your head turns to see an eagle swoop down and pluck a salmon from a wave. Or how a hockey arena holds its collective breath when Connor McDavid crosses the blue line at top speed. It is built into us to stop and notice when there's nothing getting in the way of potential coming out to play. All we have to do is take it in. It's as if their genius dilates our learning pores so that we can soak up what's happening in front of us. We give our full attention to what is emerging in the here and now.

As we start noticing more closely than we normally would, we start imagining what it must feel like to be capable of that thing. We imagine ourselves inside that experience: We mouth the lyrics, our wrists start to stickhandle, our fingers shape-shift into talons. We experience ourselves being excellent. Our brain maps on to our subject's experience, and we start creating the neural pathways to do it that way. It sends impulse after impulse faster and faster down these pathways, wiring them in. By experiencing the talent of another, we prepare ourselves for practising towards it.

In writing this, I am realizing that my life has been blessed with the opportunity to meet, share time with and notice many remarkable people who have literally shaped the way my brain works because of what I saw them do (and still see). The way they listen, the way they hold space, the way they negotiate, the way they show kindness in a tricky moment. Most of my system for leading comes from emulating people who were excellent at it. For any of us wanting to be mentors, this is an important invitation to becoming an example of excellence.

Being an Example

Rod Stewart Liddon, a friend and mentor of mine, was a crofter on the Isle of Skye. His active lifestyle made him uncharacteristically strong for his advancing age. When you shook hands with him you could feel each one of the twenty-seven bones in your hand. Rod sported a signature straw-laced ruckus of white hair that did not see a comb between pillow and early-morning chores. A keen observer of politics at home and abroad, Rod would often fire off carefully crafted letters to the editor to local and national newspapers, on topics from misconduct in the military to funding the revitalization of the Gaelic language. Sometimes the responses to his letters would be pointed and insulting, but Rod was undaunted.

He was an interesting person to be near, mostly because he was genuinely interested in the people around him. He was the sort of person who drew your attention in a room; something about his nature was distinctly solid, steady and still. He had nothing to prove to anyone. All of this left you feeling safe—even if what you were addressing with him was uncomfortable.

Rod's signature presence was hard-earned in a variety of life settings. Rod worked with young offenders in Canada and was a partner in founding the John Ridgway School of Adventure in Scotland, a mountain and sea expeditionary learning centre for youth at risk. Rod lived for over a decade in the Persian Gulf and could communicate at a basic level in Arabic. He retired to the Isle of Skye—or more accurately re-fired a new chapter—as a learner of the Gaelic language, a crofter and a mediator.

In a day and age when we so often get to know so-called leaders by what they say, Rod had an exceptional ability to communicate through his presence. If you wanted to learn from Rod, all you had to do was notice the way he conducted himself in situations. He had the Athena Signature emanating from every cell.

I first met Rod sitting with my children next to him at church. I have never known anyone, before or since, who prayed quite the way Rod Liddon did: head bowed down over clasped hands and some very deep and audible breaths. In whatever he was communicating—whatever he was giving up, or receiving—it was occurring through an unmediated relationship between him and his Maker. He had noticed our accents and introduced himself after Mass, keen to hear what had brought me from Canada to the Isle of Skye. He explained that he'd been involved with several leadership development initiatives around the world and would be happy to help at our centre if we ever needed him.

Which, of course, we did.

Rod had a natural ability to focus people's hearts and minds. It was his gift, and when he used it you couldn't help but watch what happened in the room. You could take the most distracted, frenetic and unpredictable group of teenagers from Glasgow, put them in a room with Rod for fifteen minutes, and they would emerge as focused and decisive as a crew of paramedics. He was quiet most of the time—the kind of quiet you didn't mind being around. It was in that poise and calm that he earned the trust of people from almost the very first moment. I saw Rod's presence have a remarkable effect on people over and over again, providing a number of moments that I am still emulating.

I knew that Rod had been in the military, but not much more than that. Until the day I asked him for a copy of his bio.

It was not like Rod to be late in responding to a request. So when my bio request went unanswered—twice—I was surprised. I mentioned it to him over coffee that I really needed a paragraph about him to include in a proposal. An hour later, a page with the following text arrived on my desk:

> Rod Liddon's career has spanned forty years, several continents and a range of appointments and projects. The vast majority of his work has required a high standard of leadership and contingency planning. The hour-by-hour management of sensitive operations with fast-changing scenarios, constricted by critical timings and tight deadlines has been a major part of his experience. Many of his specific roles were of a politically sensitive nature and are covered by the Official Secrets Act.

Most of my system for leading comes from emulating people who were excellent at it.

———————————

My eyes widened. I knew Rod was an interesting person, but now I knew he was *very* interesting.

As a way of sharing his gifts, he soon began running experiential learning sessions for our groups in ethics, decision-making and problem-solving. Each week on Skye, Rod would do this by leading a search-and-rescue simulation with the very wide range of clients we put in front of him: young leaders from tough socio-economic realities, injured soldiers, financial executives, head and deputy head teachers. In each simulation, with each group of people, Rod always arrived prepared and clear about how the work he was going to do with people would make them more capable of leading in their own lives.

On one occasion, it wasn't a simulation. A young local boy had gone missing. This news soon brought the community to the family's doorstep. As the police talked to relatives and the boy's friends, a crowd gathered in our centre's parking lot, which adjoined the family's driveway. There was an awkward inertia. We didn't know what to do first. We didn't know what it was time for.

Rod's arrival announced itself. "The Major's here" whispered through the group like a grassfire. He walked slowly up the driveway to the centre. The atmosphere changed when he got there, and our capability as a community changed with it.

He found out what people knew about the situation. He asked them to describe what they had said a little more, then repeated it back to them. He spoke privately with the boy's brother a few steps away from the crowd to find out more. He opened up a map of the area on the hood of his truck, and people started to gather. From time to time he asked someone if they could take a few people with them to check out a certain area where the boy might be and report back. They would dart off as Rod made a note in the little black book he carried in his back pocket.

Contrary to his nickname, his influence was not in his position, or in any authority or expertise. He had a focus and a quiet conviction that people started emulating within minutes of meeting him. His tone became our tone with each other, his focus became ours, his pace became ours.

Later that afternoon, one of our colleagues found the boy sitting on the edge of a cliff above the ocean and walked him safely home. A positive outcome—made possible by Rod's signature state in approaching us as a group, and the situation, with a clear strategy.

Knowing You Are an Example

As humble and unassuming as Rod was, he was highly aware of the example he brought to situations. He knew that he set the tone and that people emulated the way he approached things.

One afternoon, Rod shared a story with a group of new merchant navy officers about being an example. In his story the task was the fairly routine practice the British Army had in Northern Ireland during the peak of the troubles there: showing up to a village in the early-morning hours to search family homes for weapons, explosives or anything documenting plans of organized violence against the British forces by the Irish Republican Army (IRA).

Hours before sunrise, a squadron of soldiers would knock on the door of an unsuspecting household. Old and young alike would be hauled out of their beds and made to stand in the cold morning air, under guard, while other soldiers thoroughly searched the premises. Cabinets would be emptied, rafters exposed, floorboards removed. When evidence was uncovered, arrests and complications ensued. When no evidence was found, the squadron would simply move on to make their next uninvited "visit."

There are different ways a team can execute a strategy like this.

Some commanders would allow some momentum-building fervour in advance of a house search. Soldiers might wear extra gear or cover parts of their face. They might tell jokes, or share stories about past "visits," or sing sectarian songs to create a sense of unity. The point was to make the job ahead slightly easier by othering those who this was being done to. It was a natural response: They needed to get up the steam to do something unpleasant, even if it carried the risk of escalating and spilling over into violence. Which it had a tendency to do—sometimes to tragic ends.

When he was commander, Rod never allowed the jokes, the stories or the songs. He knew they represented the beginnings of a pattern that could escalate—a pattern he wanted no part of. Those things were not part of his duty or the mission at hand. He was a man who believed in the power of ethos and the necessity of ethics. Whenever possible, his soldiers removed their helmets on entry. Their searches were just as thorough, but Rod made sure, personally, that everything searched was put back the way it had been found. It's not as if household members loved having Rod and his soldiers search their house. But they must have noticed how professional his approach was.

There's a twist: Rod was Catholic. His humane-as-possible approach to his responsibilities was criticized during and after his career as overly sympathetic to the IRA cause. "Naive," they said. Even "weak." Rod didn't pay that criticism much mind. His teams had a record that was both impeccable in terms of tasks accomplished and in its avoidance of unnecessarily escalated incidents.

His way became their way. They saw how he did it, and that's how they did it.

TACTIC Making TED Requests

If I ever feel a little lost in a conversation, TED is a nice ace to keep up my sleeve. I can count on TED to help me figure out where to go next in the exchange. TED is an acronym for three requests I can make:

- "Tell me ..."
- "Explain to me ..."
- "Describe to me ..."

You'll notice these aren't questions at all, even though they're 100 percent powered by curiosity. They are requests, but they function like questions, eliciting valuable details based on something interesting a person has said. TED works particularly well with the engaging phrases and metaphors of the tactic in chapter 2:

- "Tell me about 'quirky.'"
- "Explain to me what 'doing better' would look like."
- "Describe to me what this 'battle' and getting 'hammered down' feels like."

Mentors have the great quality of not assuming they know what their mentee means (even if they do) while also asking for some evidence behind any claims their mentee is making. They have a methodical way of moving down the corridor and knocking on the doors where the important intel lies.

Emulating Example

In leadership challenges, the specifics of the situations you face will always differ from what someone else has experienced. But the way they faced things can come with you. And can even become your way.

One group we hosted on Skye was *The Big Issue*, a newspaper and social enterprise giving those facing homelessness "a hand up, not a handout." Today it is a world-renowned operation advocating for change, wraparound service provision and its core and most well-known activity: publishing and distributing a vendor-sold newspaper.

Of course, homelessness isn't a simple or solitary problem to solve. Trauma, abuse, stigma, mental health and addiction are intertwined in this complex issue. There's a lot of courage and creativity every day at *The Big Issue*. There is laughter, but there's also a lot of heartbreak.

The *Big Issue* group visiting us were seasoned veterans of living rough. As part of a pilot program to help experienced vendors take on more senior roles in the organization, this group carried with them the scars of the very hard roads their lives had been down. They also carried the buoyant grit and humour Glasgow is known for. The members of the contingent were at different stages of addressing, working on and living through their addictions.

Addiction to hard drugs shows itself in the realm of the physical. It twists the frame of the human body. It scrambles natural rhythms of sleep and energy. It aches and it groans out loud. It's hard to witness, and difficult for the untrained heart to be with. The arrival of this group on Skye had made the local community very nervous.

Two nights into a seven-day program, we got thrown a curveball.

Our caretaker phoned me at home early in the morning and asked me to come down to the centre as soon as I could. I met him outside the front door, and we walked towards the parking lot together. My heart sank as we approached the first of our two vans. Broken

Mentorship starts with example. It is where all learning begins.

---

glass crunched under our feet. We peered through the smashed driver-side window to see a nest of wires ripped out from under the dash. The glove compartment yawned open, its contents thrown around the cab. I felt a rising sense of personal insult. I had personally pitched for these vans as a gift from one of our important donors. This sort of vandalism was rare in our village; it was the sort of thing that happened in the city. The shock of seeing the first van solidified into anger as we approached the second. More shattered glass and damage—and exponentially harder feelings.

The police arrived to take a look and make a report. Everyone on our team felt unnerved and disappointed. In the midst of our demanding days, this was really the last thing we needed. Wrapped around this incident with the vans were some uncomfortable questions about whether our centre's whole approach was working, or even what the *Big Issue* participants needed.

Having police cars outside our premises got people around town talking. Rumours started that the *Big Issue* group had probably been looking for drugs. Local folks thought it was a shame that they would break into the same vans that had brought them up from Glasgow. Some were alarmed that we had brought a risk like this into their village without more information, and some wanted the group to be held accountable and for their program to end. People wanted a decision made—and they looked to me to make it.

I asked the group's chaperone, the executive director, if we could talk.

I shouldn't have been surprised with how understanding Jim Brown was of the situation I was in. He knew I was feeling pressure from every direction to take action on this. He understood that people were scared of his group. He said that if I wanted to call it quits, he would understand.

He also knew his group. Before he left my office, he explained three things that I needed to know. First, his group members would know that the glove compartment of a leadership centre's van probably didn't have anything too interesting in it. Second, he reminded me to notice their energy over the course of the days they had been on Skye. A combination of hearty highland meals, warm beds, fresh air and their medication had the group members closing their eyes for a nap at any opportunity. Breaking windows and ripping out wiring was an expenditure of energy they were not interested in. Lastly, he was cool with whatever call I had to make, but he wanted me to know that his group had *not* done this.

The window of time for sending them unceremoniously down the road was closing. And letting them stay another night was going to be seen as a weak non-decision on my part.

Rod Liddon was one of the instructors that week. He knew I was under pressure to make a call. Having seen Jim finish our meeting, he knocked on the door of my office. He wanted to see where I was at.

"One of those days?" His tone was casual, but his eyes were watching every move on my face.

In the short term, I didn't have enough information to make a decision. In the long term, I needed this community and my team to know that I was prepared to make a tough call when required.

"I think it's great that you talked with Jim," he said. "Don't get too concerned about what decision other people want you to make. They don't have all the information that you have. You'll know when it's time to make the call."

His words helped me realize that this was not the time to send them on their way. The program would continue.

This was not a popular decision in the community, or even on my team. Some team members thought it was a no-brainer because the break-in happened just thirty-six hours after the group had arrived. Believing that I was going to step up and send them home to Glasgow, the staff had already organized other plans outside work for the rest of the week. I felt the scrutiny.

And I found myself counting on the way Rod would face this kind of pressure.

As is always likely to happen in a small island village, another tidbit of intel came our way the next morning. Two local residents had taken it upon themselves to make it look like the *Big Issue* group had vandalized our vans. For years they had disapproved of our work and the groups we were bringing to their community. They wanted to complicate our efforts and this was their opportunity. They wanted the *Big Issue* people sent home. My guess is they thought they were turning the community against us.

Their mean-spirited plan almost worked. And it *would* have worked had we not had a mentor like Rod Liddon in the mix as an example, demonstrating to us a hundred times a day what it means to stay poised under pressure.

For a long time, I've watched the impact mentors have in their community. Wherever I go, the Athena Signature seems to be focused on twisting the golden rule:

Do unto others as you would have them do unto… *others*.

What these mentors do is not transactional. It's transformational. They set the tone for all of the interactions around them. Every action they take is a demonstration of the kind of leadership they would like to see more of in the world. They provide an example that others can emulate, with a bit of practice. They create a way. Like Rod did.

Like Athena did.

At the interface where their character meets the world, their conduct is practice, prayer and poem, creating community and culture in every moment.

Mentorship starts with example. It is where all learning begins.

TACTIC **Reflecting Back What You Hear**

The most impactful phrase doesn't always have to be something you create. Sometimes, the finest thing you can share is a summary of what you've heard. Reflecting back—whether in personal or professional relationships—is an underused yet highly effective strategy to help the person you're speaking with understand how they're carrying their challenge around. It subtly and powerfully meets people where they're at.

It's almost too easy. And it *always* works.

If your reflection back to the person in front of you feels 100 percent accurate to them, they'll feel confirmed and heard. If your reflection only hits 80 percent of the target, fine. They'll fill in the other 20 percent. And even if your summary is completely off-base, they'll automatically correct it and articulate themselves better. You can't go wrong.

Often it's advantageous if a mentor uses "clean" language in their reflection. That means only using words and phrases that the mentee has used in the conversation. It's a way of honouring your mentee.

Mentee: There's just too much expected of me. I'm expected to create new content, lead the team meetings and keep us all organized, support individual team members and sell enough to hit our revenue targets.

Mentor: It sounds like between creating content, leading the team, supporting individuals and selling, that people are expecting too much from you?

In other instances, it may make sense to reframe what you've heard and introduce new language in your summary that captures the nuances and feelings you're picking up on. It also helps a mentee gain perspective on how they're coming across.

Mentee: There's just too much expected of me. I'm expected to create new content, lead the team meetings and keep us all organized, support individual team members and sell enough to hit our revenue targets.

Mentor: It sounds like on any given day, people are counting on you to touch four very different functions?

Accurate or not—their words or your summary—reflecting back what you've heard is the sign of a pro.

REFLECTION

- What are three specific behaviours from the example you set that you would like others to emulate?

MEDITATION
Notice What Is Being Learned

Notice what is being learned.
What of this learning is coming from you.
And what learning is coming from them.
The intentional and the unintentional.
If you catch yourself being impressive—
stop immediately.

Notice what is being learned.
You are not the teacher.
Experience is the teacher.
Their experience of you is part of it—
but not all of it.
It was never supposed to work that way.

Notice what is being learned.
Learning is a journey from within.
Risking the chance to meet new experience,
our pores wide open to new awareness and new focus.

Crafting how we meet the moment over and over again.
Learning needs a reason why.

Notice what is being learned.
Plunging into our desire to be more,
churning away through the icy waves,
away from the mainland we know
to strange and confusing islands.
Where one would be wise to act differently.

Notice what is being learned.
Again and again—committing to our practice.
Some days we are keen—some days we are not.
Until that one morning when a beautiful sandbar
has emerged between who we have always been
and who we are capable of being now.

Notice what is being learned.
What visceral sense of right action
has begun to make itself at home
deep in the guts of this person?
How acutely will they feel this sense again?
And what will they choose if they do not?

8

Focus on Learning, Not Teaching

The purpose of learning is to increase our abilities to recognize the complexities of situations, and to help us develop increasingly nuanced and sophisticated strategies for acting and responding.

MARY HELEN IMMORDINO-YANG & ANTONIO DAMASIO

LEARNING IS a tender topic for me.

I've spent my professional career focused on the learning of others, but have a very unpredictable relationship when it comes to my own learning. I've tended to focus on doing things I'm naturally strong at rather than pursue new areas of learning. I stretch myself with how far I can go on the paths that are known to me—it's more like endurance running than pathfinding new or adjacent areas of interest.

So writing this chapter feels quite personal.

I found that so-called learning in high school came quite easily to me. I listened in class and could forecast what would probably be on the exam. As selective as it might be, I also have a good memory.

Learning at university was a different story. I wasn't hungry to study or research; I was hungry to do things. A university exchange year in Scotland gave me the kind of immersion I was looking for: gross anatomy labs, bartending in the evenings, living life to the fullest. When I failed to get into medical school I was drawn into the world of work, where my appetite to learn from experience—diving into leadership development experiences and finding a creative way through the inevitable challenges—went into overdrive. I was also in my early 20s, so I had buckets of energy and loved work. I liked the way it consumed me. I loved having responsibility for outcomes, and all the relationship and conceptual prowess that this responsibility required and developed in me.

Informal teaching felt like an extension of this. In commanding the attention of a room full of people, I found something I was good at. I could connect with the audience and share game-changing ideas simultaneously. The way I explained things seemed to really land with people. I liked keeping things on track. It felt good to teach, and having wiped out in my applications to medical schools, it also felt good to be good at something. So I kept doing it. I took every opportunity to get better and better at it. My experience of teaching in all its forms—instructing, briefing simulations, convening conversations and even writing—was something I loved crashing into. And still do. Writing this chapter will require interrogating an experience that I love.

The Temptation to Teach

It's no wonder that our urge to share what we know is a trademark of our initial desires to be mentors. I've read hundreds of applications to mentorship programs, and "to share my experience" is the reason most frequently listed by people to explain why they would like to be involved.

This is not new. Mentor himself was a teacher. He was smart, focused and disciplined in the way he thought and the way he taught. I'm guessing he was well known as a good teacher because Penelope and Odysseus chose him to be a resource to their son. But it didn't get the job done.

Whether we like it or not, our ego is wrapped up in our desire to teach. There's a reason older siblings everywhere like to play school and take on the role of the teacher. There is something so satisfying about desking our younger siblings. It was probably the way we experienced our first taste of adulthood. Playing school put us in the position of being a professional, of having some authority. We liked the idea of being a big deal. We liked the idea of helping others be better. And we still love having a sense of control to get things done, on our terms. In a wild, wild world, who can blame us for wanting to take some control?

Control lies at the heart of many professions, but most significantly for our conversation here, the profession and function of teaching. Let's not kid ourselves, though. It's not just teachers who want control. It's parents. It's partners. It's anyone who has been a child, a student or a lover, or has been jealous, watched a project flounder in someone else's hands or felt lonely or afraid.

That's all of us. And that's why releasing control is such a panic-inducing idea.

The difference between teaching and learning is an important distinction for mentors to understand and be aware of at all times. A focus on teaching involves looking at the process through the lens of the person who hopes to absorb someone else's learning. It's about choosing which concepts need to be introduced and the lesson plan for introducing them. It's about setting up the space around learners to be conducive for a transfer of knowledge. It's about making choices around what you want them to know, and how you will share that. Teaching is ultimately a series of decisions that determine how someone else will learn.

Great instruction is an important component in the creation of impactful learning. I often find examples outside of the formal profession to be the best at illustrating what great teaching looks like: A seasoned wildfire incident commander uses a set briefing method to invite multiple teams to update the wider group on their efforts to evacuate communities in the path of a massive blaze; a data scientist uses international ship records from a period of 315 years to animate the Atlantic slave trade in a video that lasts two minutes; a successful entrepreneur takes to the stage at a networking mixer to tell the story of their most colossal mistake. These are all examples of the power of a commanding presence, conceptual prowess and storytelling—the cornerstones of great teaching.

But they are ingredients. The learning they create is the stew. The change of perspectives, the grasping of magnitude, the awareness of context that these stirrings create are what mentors need to be paying attention to.

This focus on learning demands an insatiable curiosity about what's happening inside other people. What experience do they bring to this moment? What are they capable of today? What are the conditions that elicit this capacity? What would they like to be capable of tomorrow? What are they prepared to sacrifice to make that happen? How many repetitions will they need before seeing significant progress? What are they taking away from their experience? What are they leaving behind? Ignited by our curiosity, the learner becomes more aware of where they are today and what they might be capable of in the future.

Learning is what will make our mentees able to do more the next time they face challenges and dilemmas.

This nuanced, disciplined and selfless shift of focus and control—from oneself to another—is yet another application of the Athena Signature. Our focus must be on the experience that's in front of our mentee more than on our own. Our focus must be on what *they* are leading through—not on what *we* accomplished, even in similar situations. It's about their learning, not our teaching.

Mentors who can shift and maintain their focus in this way will be invaluable in assisting leaders navigate an increasingly complex future. When contexts become unpredictable, leaders are still required to make ground.

In a complex system, the connections between factors are too numerous or too hidden to discern. No one knows what the right way forward is. There is no best practice to be taught. Leaders can only learn the right way forward as it emerges, and that involves the design of several *different* paths, as well as being clear about what will constitute early indications of success and failure. A team may have to try ten ways forward to find the one that works. When one of these probes starts to work, we can amplify it. When a probe shows indications of not working, we can dampen or even eliminate it.

Mentors who show up to support learning rather than teach will equip our next generation of leaders with the confidence and the example- and sense-making capabilities they require. They learn to see the endless possibilities inherent when they show up present to what's really happening, rather than being told how to behave in a specific situation, a type of learning that's protracted and non-transferable. They trust their own ability to choose a course of action in the moment, rather than depending on what you tell them they should do. They learn to turn inward for the answers, rather than seeking to satisfy a mentor's recommendations. They learn how to re-find the future, over and over again, as many times as is required.

Those of us unable to shift our focus away from the value of our own experience might very well find that people have had their fill of our clever sound bites, heroic stories and name-dropping. It isn't hard to understand why anyone would choose to connect with people who are practised and disciplined in creating space for their companions, rather than taking up all of the space themselves.

Experience Is *the* Teacher

The teacher in me loves sharing concepts with people: stories, models, tools, theories, ideas. The realm of the conceptual is interesting and can be liberating. Put the right tool in the hands of a leader who needs it, and they'll be grateful for your help for a long time.

For years, our business has prided itself on putting concepts from the tool boxes of professional coaches, negotiators and facilitators into the hands of the everyday leaders who make things happen in the world. Our concepts have produced a confidence to practise in thousands of leaders. We've become very strong at this half of the equation.

Where Roy Group is raising its game is in the sphere of the *emergent*: being present to help leaders learn as much as they can from their own practice. This work—the perceptual—is less polished and less predictable. These are uncomfortable discussions about what has worked and what hasn't, but the effort aligns with this powerful statement on where the real learning happens:

Experience is *the* teacher.

If there's one core belief that has deepened in me without any special effort, it's that leaders learn most from their own experience. They find themselves addressing situations that are bigger than they are: a new role, a new geography, an audacious new chapter of their enterprise. They immediately start clocking as much of the context around them as they possibly can, noticing the personalities, tracking the trends, sensing where the momentum to make things happen resides. They find their feet, their voice and their focus. They make connections and establish credibility with others. They negotiate a way forward. They have a meaningful experience—inside and out—and take as much learning as they can from it.

Ask a leader where they learned how to lead and they'll undoubtedly tell you "along the way." This learning may have been amplified by a great workshop or program over the years, but at the core, leaders must make sense of the situations in front of them and weave together what it all means—about themselves, others and the community—on their own. And it's in this weaving together of meaning that mentors find their most valuable assignments.

Sometimes, your presence will help someone make sense of what's happened: winning a contract that will evolve their business; a frustrating interaction where they lost their temper; the loss of a team member. Good news or bad, these are the experiences that leaders learn the most from.

But the fast-paced nature of modern work and the unrelenting demands on leaders compromise how much learning their experience provides them. A mentor's role is to carve out time and slow the pace so that a thorough weave of sense-making can take place. What has this leader learned about the world? What have they learned about others? What have they learned about themselves?

At other times, your presence will be required for the delicate work of pulling the weave apart: helping someone return to what they made an experience mean, and creating some space in the

Experience is
the teacher we learn
from the most.

---

warp and weft of it all to help someone realize that more learning was available. For example, the excitement of a new promotion also comes with some steep political risks. And cutting ties with a long-term colleague can be perceived as an act of protection of the company's culture. The frustration a leader feels about their role becomes a mindful awareness of what their gift as a leader is, and the realization that their role doesn't allow them to use it.

These multi-layered realities aren't positive or negative. They just are. But when leaders become more aware of them, they can make a better choice going forward. Mentors help leaders become more aware of how they carry what's happened, and more discerning about how they move forward. They deepen just how much experience shapes a leader. But experience is *the* teacher. At best, our place as mentors is as the teacher's capable assistants.

Our apprenticeship to experience never really ends. Our role is to provide what's required for people to learn as much as they can from it.

Being Authentic Means Being Incomplete

When I was first introduced to coaching as a skill, it didn't feel very authentic to me. I had a profound respect for the people who gave me a chance to practise, but every time I did, it felt like they were throwing me into the ocean and telling me to swim out to an island. On this island, a person was expected to conduct themselves in a grounded, measured, curious and patient way, all in the service of someone else's deep reflection.

It was a departure from the mainland of my authentic self.

When I was just being me, I didn't act this way. I was impulsive and would say outrageous things. I liked taking action. I loved to tell stories, and I loved distracting others and myself with humour. Seriously, I was a pretty good time.

So being highly aware of my every word—and paying attention to what a person was explaining rather than what I was thinking—was a long, cold stretch to swim. Once I got there, it felt like I was putting on a cloak and acting like someone else. This was simply not the way I would naturally conduct myself.

Until the day it was.

I don't remember the exact circumstances, only that by practising over and over again I had readied myself to make the swim to Coach Island—and one day there suddenly appeared a sandbar bridging who I was and what I'd been working on. Now it was authentic to be outrageous and fun, and it also felt authentic to coach a team with focus, attention and care.

Now, it was all me. Being a work in progress had made me more than I was before.

We must be careful not to conceive of a mentor as being a *fait accompli*. Mentors have not arrived at the destination; they have not yet met their full greatness. They're learning and evolving beings like any of us. Any mentor who falls into the trap of believing that their value comes from what they've accomplished is less valuable than the one who can still speak to what they're in the midst of accomplishing. Any mentor who's stopped learning, convinced that their collection of lessons learned to date is sufficient to inspire, is missing the bull's eye of impact. Mentors who default to a proven collection of one-liners aren't creating the space for the real conversations people want to have with them.

Mentors who know and share the ways they are incomplete—what they're working on and learning and creating, as well as where they're coming up short—invite us into the journey alongside them. They enable us to be everything we are, plus everything we aren't quite, yet.

TACTIC Negotiating Assignments

Mentors help others shape the kinds of experiences they can learn from. When the theme of a mentee's learning and development comes up, a mentor can help to negotiate a learning assignment. In addition to setting up what is required, this involves the mentee working outside the time constraints of your conversations, maximizing its value.

For example, you might want the mentee to interview three people about a certain topic, or to create a one-page learning plan for the year ahead. Try introducing it this way: "I'd like to craft an assignment *with* you. You can take this assignment or leave it. You can also negotiate the details to make it just right. Let's craft a piece of homework that you're keen to take on."

REFLECTION

- What are ten things you would like to learn more about in becoming a better mentor?

MEDITATION
Be Judicious with What You Share

Be judicious with what you share.
We know how lavish your wealth of experience feels,
and how profoundly relevant
each piece seems in the moment.
We know just how good it would feel to share.
Your uncommon lessons were hard won.

Be judicious with what you share.
Do not give in to the desire to shape
this piece that they are working on.
They may play this differently than you did.
They may play this differently than you would.
They may play this differently than you ever could.

Be judicious with what you share.
The illuminated pattern that they face now,
that maps so uncannily over the one you faced,
has different, invisible and uncompromisable dimensions.

You would be wise to hold your fire.
You would be wise to find out more.

Be judicious with what you share.
Notice your advice appearing.
Even note it down.
Categorize it and put it in order.
Prepare yourself to share it all.
Even though you know you won't.

Be judicious with what you share.
Your presence is not lessened by your curiosity.
Your credibility is not at stake if you are quiet.
Your advice will not expire if it is held and tempered.
Your value does not come from the quantity you offer.
And understanding is not the same as agreeing.

Be judicious with what you share.
Distill all of your advice down to its essence.
Spell out the one strong steer
that you know will help someone
see the opportunity or the pitfall
that they are running blindly towards.

9

Your Advice Is Worth Less (Than You Think)

People don't care how much you know, until they know how much you care.
THEODORE ROOSEVELT

ONE OF the most exciting moments in mentorship is when we feel we have some sage advice to offer. The pattern that the person across the table from us is describing overlaps with a pattern we recognize. Pattern recognition is exhilarating—*now we're in this together!* We know where this story goes, and we can't wait to provide them with a heads-up.

It feels so good to help.

Moments like this line up with our mental model of what being a mentor is all about: sharing our experience. When we first started to imagine ourselves as mentors, many of us probably equated that role with being a trusted advisor, using our expertise and judgment to guide other people through. We come to sound conclusions. We brim with ideas and prescriptions other people should use. This is our chance to provide some evidence that we're savvy and seasoned. And it's so much easier to solve other people's problems than our own. We equate our mentee's need to find a way forward with our desire to help them do what *we* would do.

How can this be anything but great?

We shift into advice mode in an unconscious second and hear ourselves launching in with statements like:

"Have you ever thought about…"

"I faced this very same thing…"

"You know what you need to do?…"

"I've been there and…"

And at that very moment, if you're paying attention, you can sense a slight constriction around the neck of the conversation. Because you haven't been there—not to *their* there, you haven't. The exact moment we're convinced we have the answers to another leader's problem is the moment that we need to hold ourselves back.

On the receiving end of the advice, the other person knows that what you're saying is probably valuable. Maybe they sense a sweet surrender of responsibility: Someone else just hopped into the pilot's seat! Or they politely nod and affirm the advice you've offered, doing their best to look like they're seriously considering your counsel. But inside, their arms cross and an eyebrow goes up. They're a little skeptical of your certainty about their situation.

If it was this simple to solve, they're thinking, *don't you think I would have done it?*

Instead, the social contract compels them to say, "That's a really good perspective. Thank you."

Of course, everyone can get better at receiving advice. And other people don't tell us what to do as much as it feels like. They're not intending to make the story of our life feel "less than" by sharing a story of theirs. Life is a nuanced operation, and there's truth in all of our stories. The more lines of sight in any situation, the better, right? We would all be wise to have people around us who can help us read the tea leaves of our existence.

Just maybe with a bit more method.

We can also consciously improve the way we provide advice. Advice isn't wrong; it can be incredibly valuable. Like everything else in this book, what the advice *is* matters less than how it's brought to the table.

The Big Lobster Claw

Any lobster has one big claw and one smaller claw. The big claw is big because they use it often for the heavy lifting: hunting, and crushing stuff. The smaller claw gets used less, and for more discreet tasks: tearing things, eating, sorting. Remembering this helps in finding a better way of giving advice—because we have two claws, too.

Our big claw is our tendency to *tell*.

We use it to tell people what they need to know and need to do. Sometimes we even tell people what they need to *be*. Our big claw isn't afraid to throw things around a little to get them moving in the right direction. It's quick and it's effective.

Our big claw is big because it's had a lot of training. We've been taught to use it from a young age.

In kindergarten, they let us explore the room and explore the day. No big challenges and no serious consequences. Soon, we enter Grade 1 and take a seat in our little wooden leg-cage to start "real" school. Questions come from the front, and if we have the answer, we raise our big claw. If we're clever, we raise it faster and higher than anyone else. We are conditioned to believe that the bigger and faster our big claw, the more valuable we are to the system we find ourselves in. And that really starts to pump it up.

We cruise through grade after grade. "Will this be on the test?" becomes our main question so that our big claw can be ready with the right answers. We dabble with a vocation or two and seek out gaining some form of technical expertise, which in turn makes us able to tell people what the answers to problems are. This makes us valuable. If we keep coming up with the answers, we get paid.

Our big claw also gives us that same sense that tempts us to teach: control. And one way to get control is to do everything ourselves. This allows us to complete tasks exactly how we like them completed, and probably gets us our first few promotions. We do good work. We get put in control of bigger pieces. And we get put in control of other people.

The moment we're convinced we have the answers to another leader's problem is exactly when we need to hold ourselves back.

The next best thing to doing everything the way we like is to clearly tell someone else how they need to do it. The big claw didn't just power us through school—it's now going to power us through our career. We're all set for a big-claw life!

Is it any wonder we're so ready to use our big claw and give people our advice?

Or that our mental model of being a mentor is about being an advisor?

And what's so wrong with giving people the benefit of our advice, anyway?

The Story We've Never Heard

Roy Group has collected many stories about people who have earned the word *mentor*, and a solid fraction of those stories are about advice: How, at exactly the right time and place, a mentor saw a pattern in the mentee's life and counselled them accordingly. The two most common kinds of stories involve a mentor sending people towards an opportunity they didn't see, or away from a brick wall they didn't know they were approaching at speed.

But there is one story we've never heard:

"My mentor is incredible. The sheer quantity of advice they have at the ready is astounding. They only need to listen to me for a few moments before they start mapping out what I need to do. I'm so grateful. I don't know what I'd do without them."

Hundreds of stories collected and not a single account like this one. It's obviously not about the quantity or readiness of the advice. It's about the quality of advice, and the mentor's ability to choose the guidance we actually need from all that they could provide.

When advice is sparing and well thought out, people pay attention to it. When it is relevant and useful, people use it. When it is deeply informed by the life circumstances of the person being advised, it hits home.

But otherwise? More than likely it's not welcome.

All this is at odds with the internal experience of wanting to provide advice. We love giving advice. It comes from an inexhaustible wellspring of insights and intuition. It brings to mind all the patterns, characters and stories in our own life that, in the moment, we believe represent some kind of answer. What we really want to do is launch into a solution with the zeal of a twelve-year-old who knows how to solve a Rubik's cube.

But we need to learn how to take it another way.

Directive Approach Versus Non-Directive Approach

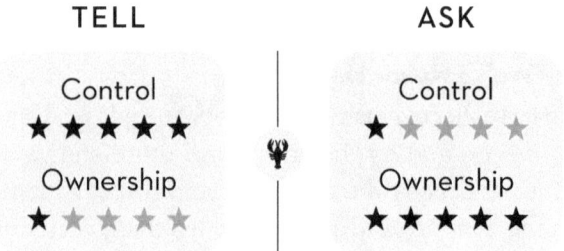

The Little Lobster Claw

Enter the little claw.

Our little lobster claw is our ability to *ask*.

It's small because we don't use it as often. We use it quite naturally when an experience is brand new, such as exploring somewhere we've never been before. But because we don't like to send a message to the world that we don't fully understand something, we tend to use our little claw with a bit of reluctance.

Leveraging our little claw is so important in mentorship, though, that I've dedicated much of this chapter and chapter 12 to it. If we learn how to use it well, the gift words of *mentor*, *leader* and *collaborator* are going to be flying off the shelves. Using our little claw well is also the surprising key to our big claw offering advice that actually gets used.

In those moments when we can't hold our big claw back, we suffer from a combination of myopia, bias and a control addiction. We're making the potentially dangerous assumption that this person's situation is (or was) the same as ours. The chances of this are actually slim. We're also rolling right into an assumption that they should do what we would do.

This is the moment when you need to take your insatiable desire for control over what other people need to do and channel it into some sovereignty over how you proceed. Sense your vocal cords readying themselves to contribute. Take a nice, slow breath in and keep listening. Forgive yourself—but also hold yourself back. Invite yourself to understand just a bit more about what the person is explaining to you—both the conversation and the gaps where advice might help, if ripened. Instead of sliding into your own story, stay with theirs. Notice something new that you haven't noticed before: the words they're repeating, the change in their tone of voice, the part of this they *aren't* talking about.

We need to conduct ourselves as if we've never come across a situation or a person like this before. We need to clarify the details and confirm any assumptions we might be bringing. We need to get over ourselves and back into what's being shared.

If, in these moments, we can stir our own curiosity about all the ways this person's situation is different from ours, our little claw will start working its magic. We'll begin to craft questions that help identify differences even within the overlap between our experience and theirs. This understanding can season and contextualize our perspective.

The more we ask, the more we understand what the other person is actually facing. The more we understand, the more we can tailor the advice we're considering dispensing. And the more we tailor it, the more refined and impactful it becomes. Of the ten pieces of advice we're initially tempted to offer, perhaps they all distill down to one: that singular bit of guidance that will actually help a person change course.

This is how the best mentors steer us in a way we'll remember and appreciate for the rest of our lives.

We all need a steer from time to time. But no one needs a know-it-all.

TACTIC WAITing

I understand how compelling it is to provide advice. I have to hold myself back, every day. I sit on my big claw sometimes just to keep it from hurting someone. As comedian and Oklahoma's favourite son Will Rogers once said, "Never miss an opportunity to shut up."

As a slightly less abrupt reminder to help my practice, I've learned to count on the acronym WAIT, which simply stands for "Why Am I Talking?" It's a really good question in all of life, not just in mentorship. Sometimes I write it in the corner of my notebook. Sometimes I mouth the words to myself. It's a discreet and non-judgmental invitation to myself to listen more, ask more, notice more and understand more.

We don't need to livestream our insights as they come. Our initial thoughts aren't going anywhere. If the advice we have on offer is as brilliant as we sense it is in the first moment we feel compelled to share it, it'll still be valuable in five minutes. If something still feels helpful after a bit of poised restraint, it probably is. If we forget it along the way, it wasn't as relevant as we first suspected.

From the stories we've collected, it's clear there are some risks involved if we don't remind ourselves with WAIT from time to time and make providing advice a conscious choice.

The secret seems to be finding a balance. In the stories we hear about mentor relationships that deteriorate and come to an end, the key reasons have to do with getting the balance wrong when it comes to advice. When the ratio of focus on the mentee's experience to focus on the mentor's gets too low, the mentee feels "less than" in the equation. The relationship weakens. Aim for a 3:1 ratio.

When the ratio of questions, curiosity and care to answers, insights and opinions gets too low, a mentee feels that answers are being pushed on them. The relationship weakens. My money's on keeping a ratio of about 4:1 here.

The great benefit of getting these ratios into a good balance is that when it's time to give some advice, you can really lay it down.

When It's Time to Lay Advice Down

In August 2004 I was alone on the Isle of Skye finishing my final month as the first CEO of the Columba 1400 International Leadership Centre. Anne-Marie and our three children had returned to Canada to set up our new life there, giving me a chance to tidy up loose ends in the transition to the new CEO.

Focus on Mentee's Experience as a Leader	Focus on Mentor's Experience as a Leader
Use of Questions, Curiosity and Care	Use of Answers, Insights and Opinions

It was a tough time for me. Some regrets had snuck in about things we hadn't accomplished at the centre. I refer to it now as a bad case of CEO-itis (which I've since realized is fairly common among senior leaders who leave their post). A strange resentment had festered to a point where people were noticing my mood and were undoubtedly looking forward to resetting the organization with a new CEO. I can imagine that I looked worn out, because I was: grey, tired and disappointed in all that had not been achieved.

Sue and Ron Myers are special mentors of mine who my brother and I first met in New York in the 1990s. They're both the kind of deeply experienced mentor that a young executive needs in their life, having advised CEOs and entrepreneurs over decades. They both enjoyed Skye, had made the trip several times and had arranged one final visit to spend a few days with me in my last month at the helm. I don't know what they saw or sensed in me, but they arranged an appointment for an afternoon in my cottage (which at this point had three wooden chairs, a toaster, a case of beer and a hockey bag with my clothes and shaving kit).

We sat down together in the front room by the peat fire—and they wasted no time in giving me the talking-to of my young life.

They identified some expressions they had overhead me saying and asked me if I was aware how often I was using them. They identified the old ideas I was clinging to as if they were the only things I would ever create and told me never to talk about them again, and to get busy creating new ones. Sue told me to stop beating myself up and looking for attention. But most of all, in their closing argument, Ron told me that what he wanted to see in me immediately—right there in that room—was an immense sense of J-O-Y for everything that *had* been accomplished on my watch. (He actually spelled it out for effect, which I thought was C-O-O-L.)

He didn't need me to brag about my accomplishments, or even talk about them, but I did have to take joy in them. If there was no room for joy, then I would have to dump something else that was taking up space inside me. And he told me to keep dumping until there was room for a boatload of J-O-Y.

The centre had helped thousands of people in its first five years. I needed to take that on. It hadn't been perfect: there had been a few missteps, I'd taken a few tough hits and I had sacrificed important things in my life for the endeavour at hand. But we made a big old dent in the universe. And that meant I had every reason to connect to joy and leave the rest behind.

Sue and Ron just wouldn't accept any other way forward.

My head went down and I knew what they were saying was true. I felt a strange mix of relief and embarrassment vying for space in my emotions. I'm not sure if what happened next was tears or laughter. Likely some raw combination. It was most certainly a release of a needless weight I'd picked up.

In the weeks ahead, my last on Skye, I reflected on all that had happened and had no choice but to admit that Sue and Ron were right and that they had helped me move on to the next chapter of my life.

I learned that day that there's a time when good friends, and trusted advisors, need to lay advice down so clearly that you are compelled to pick it up—as a strong steer in the right direction—and go forward differently.

TACTIC Noticing Patterns in Language

Mentors track where a conversation has come from and where it's headed. In addition to paying attention to what's being shared, they're also cognizant of the patterns emerging in the conversation, and when it's helpful they share what they notice transparently, without any judgment. Mentors pay close attention to the things people say, the way they express themselves and what it all might signify. People really do say the darndest things—often without even realizing what they've just said. And some phrases are just plain interesting.

Exaggerated Frequency: Sometimes people will exaggerate how often a thing happens. Statements containing *always* and *never*, or *all* and *none*, are usually worth finding out more about.

Mentee: He takes *no* responsibility for his job.

Mentor: Is there anything he does take responsibility for?

Unspoken Emotion: When people use a strong word or distinct tone to describe the emotional state they're experiencing, it's valuable to find out more.

Mentee: It has just become so ridiculous.

Mentor: Can you tell me more about what's frustrating?

Unconscious Repetition: Sometimes people will repeat a word or phrase without even realizing it. If we can track it, it's helpful to put that pattern in front of them.

Mentee: The quirkiness factor is real.

Mentor: You've used the word *quirky* four times in our conversation. What does *quirky* mean to you?

REFLECTION

- What is the single best piece of advice anyone has ever given you?

- What made this advice so valuable to you?

MEDITATION
Midwife the Triumphs of Others

Midwife the triumphs of others.
Enter the room focused and serene.
Meet each stage of discomfort with calm,
care and connection. Be with.
This is not your pain. This is not your struggle.
This is their unfolding story.

Midwife the triumphs of others.
The adventures you pursued were then.
This is now.
Every theme that deepened in you
must now uncover the themes in them
that deepen without trying.

Midwife the triumphs of others.
Hold yourself back from the challenge, itself.
The enterprise is theirs.
They are your endeavour. They are your focus.

Even and especially in their failures.
Like a bookmark to remind them where they left off.

Midwife the triumphs of others.
Your role today on this stage
is more influence than authority.
You are part of the setting.
You are a frame to the painting
that people can't stop looking at.

Midwife the triumphs of others.
Make every movement
a fierce investment in what they labour for.
Accompany them in immersing into
what it will look like and feel like when they are done—
so that they have already prevailed.

Midwife the triumphs of others.
Almost anonymously.
Your ability to recognize their moment,
prepare them for it, and ready them for it.
Be that person who makes their story come to life—
That practitioner whose name they can't quite remember.

10

It's Not About You

*There is an imperative need for the creator
in every supporting role to be able to perceive
the gravity of these roles.*

THAMBI RAMAIAH

I LIKE TO perform. I don't mean perform as in *do things well* as much as *act out*. I like saying outrageous things and showing off. If there's a play, I'm going to audition for the lead role.

I really like attention. There. I said it.

Put me in front of an audience and I'll light up. And I'll light other people up. Any trouble I got into as a kid was because a classroom is really just a captive audience for shenanigans. I was the kid who would only skate hard in the hockey rink when my mom and dad were in the stands. If they weren't there, there was just no one to perform for. Ask my teammates from that time and they'll confirm: it was pretty hot and cold. Mostly cold.

I was a kid who wore a fedora while downhill skiing and skied under the chairlift as often as I could so that people would see it. (If you're wondering how skiing works with a fedora: It doesn't.) I tend to buy unique pieces of clothing, to the extent that I've been told my eccentricity is a professional risk. As an adult, I've received strong suggestions from colleagues to take a look in the mirror before I go out and turn any weird volumes down. I was encouraged to replace interesting costume items from around the world with "business staples" that I could mix and match. More black and grey, and fewer fedoras with chin straps.

Seriously, I'm a colourful piece of work—but a piece of work *in progress*.

Over the course of becoming a full-fledged adult (a process that's still very much in progress), I began to recognize that my favourite people weren't the show-offs. They weren't wearing fedoras under the chairlift.

Rather, these people were calm and steady and grounded, and generous in the attention they gave to others. They had nothing to prove and no need to impress. They were quiet champions.

And I met many of those folks through the world of coaching.

I'm indebted to the practice of coaching mostly because it demands this discipline of remaining focused on others. I was introduced to coaching in my mid-20s and really liked the look and feel of it. I knew it was something that I actually wanted to get good at, not just look good doing.

The concept of conducting ourselves in a way that makes space for others to perform, learn and engage—whether on a rugby pitch, at a job interview or in the C-suite—is something I love introducing others to. I like helping leaders learn how to coach because it's something I myself desperately needed to learn. And something I need to keep learning about—and practising.

As I mentioned earlier, my learning curve in coaching went stratospheric when we moved to Scotland as a new family in 2000. Coaching as a leadership strategy in business was a relatively new phenomenon back in the early 2000s. At that time, it almost felt as if there was a country-wide community of practice. Some coaches were based in London, some hailed from Edinburgh, others from Glasgow, Stirling or Hertfordshire.

One distinct characteristic shared amongst those at the centre of this movement was the way they kept their focus trained on the quality of their coaching—not on themselves as coaches. It was more about their shared practice of coaching in various fields across society than becoming personal icons of the movement.

These same practitioners were excited about the work we were doing on the Isle of Skye with young people from tough socio-economic backgrounds. I was 27, a young CEO of a new organization and a prime candidate for coaching. Little did I know that over the next five years, I'd be on the receiving end of some incredible coaching, from some of the United Kingdom's most gifted practitioners. Through them, I would get to meet a wide array of people shaping the profession of coaching in the UK, and I was excited that I got to be a part of it.

A Sticky Note to Remember

One excellent practice used by this community of coaches was an exercise called "the trio," where three practitioners interact while playing three different roles—coach, coachee and supercoach—within a time-constrained period of observed performance. The actual coaching lasted twenty minutes, and a ten-minute review followed. This exercise provided newcomers like me with real-time feedback on the quality of our coaching from more seasoned practitioners.

Immediately I grasped the strength of this approach to learning: I'd receive these insights while my role as coach was still fresh in my consciousness. No matter who was sitting in the supercoach's seat that day, their feedback always landed in an impactful way, quickly helping me improve my skills.

This approach to learning a new skill is clearly mapped out by author and researcher Daniel Coyle in his 2009 book, *The Talent Code*. Close observation of performance, coupled with immediate feedback, are core elements of what Coyle calls "deep practice." Combined with a key third element—repeating the performance with an eye to using the feedback to improve on observed weaknesses—this method has been shown to enhance learning, anchoring it permanently on a cellular level in the nervous system.

Trios are an extraordinary accelerant to becoming an impactful coach, especially if the person offering feedback is someone you trust to be honest about what they see happening. Someone like Peter Hill.

Peter was the very first person I'd ever seen using coaching in the workplace. Thanks to a partnership between our two companies in the late 1990s, I had the chance to see Peter demonstrate coaching methods with individuals and teams on both sides of the Atlantic. He was also one of the first people in my professional life who gave me the sense that I was worth championing. When I accepted the CEO job at Columba, Peter was one of my first visitors to Skye, checking in on us and exploring how this new position might be a chance for me to deepen my practice of coaching.

I hadn't seen Peter for a few months. Because I held him in such high regard, I was keen to demonstrate that I'd been working at my coaching. I had that old, familiar feeling that it was time to strut my stuff. Because I'd learned so much through the trio practice, we made arrangements to do a trio during his visit. And I knew exactly who I wanted to coach.

Maggie was from Ireland, a housekeeper on our team and someone who was very clear that she wanted "a fair day's wage for a fair day's graft." She didn't want to take part in any of this other culture "bumph." But she had agreed to be in a trio and work through a real issue with me in front of Peter so that I could get some feedback on my coaching.

I don't know if she realized what she'd signed up for.

I asked Maggie about her topic the day before our trio. This gave me a chance to plan my attack. I hatched a strategy: I was going to make full use of the time we had together. I was going to take things head-on. There was going to be shock and there was going to be awe.

The next day, Maggie, Peter and I met in my office as planned. Coffees in hand, we eased into some small talk. In my mind, I was ticking the box of "building rapport."

After a few more moments, I cleared my throat and began.

I asked Maggie to sketch out her topic. I asked her to explain why it was important. I challenged her. I supported her. I interjected

Mentorship is not a status.

insightful perspectives. I pivoted. I came at it all from another direction. I applied rigorous questioning. I reflected back the interesting phrases she was using. I pointed out inconsistencies. I negotiated a seven-step action plan. I asked her to physically sign off on this plan, with a deadline beside each item.

It was incredible—I was magnificent, and I was looking forward to my feedback from Peter.

But when my conversation with Maggie ended, it felt like Peter had forgotten that we were going to go through feedback. He asked Maggie if she wanted to grab a cup of tea in the café.

"Oh, I'm surprised we aren't going to roll right into feedback while this is all still fresh," I said. By "this" I meant this masterpiece, of course.

Peter smiled, his hand on the doorknob.

"I'm going to use a slightly different feedback approach today, Chiz," he said, calling me by my nickname. "I watched you carefully for the best part of the last hour. And I've written everything you need to know about your coaching on this one sticky note."

He handed me the paper. This was the moment I'd been waiting for.

My mind raced with all the things he might have written on that little square of paper:

You are incredible.
Welcome, young Jedi.
You rock, Chiz.

I took that piece of paper and pressed it between my hands.

I had earned this. A lot of hard work had resulted in this moment, and I had shone brightly. I held that sticky note the way a child holds their last present on Christmas morning. This was going to be a keeper.

As he and Maggie headed downstairs for their tea, Peter kicked the stopper on my door so that it would close—to leave me alone, I supposed. To savour this moment I was so looking forward to.

I slapped the sticky note down on my desk, keeping a hand over it for one more breath before I looked down to read it. With a deep breath, I took my hand away.

I still have that note.

Win a Different Oscar

I wanted to be an actor when I was young.

I still daydream about it. Whether in theatre or film, how much fun it must be to make your living from acting things out. To use the things you say and the way you say them to stir emotions in people and have audiences in the palm of your hand. Having lights on you must be a wonderful warmth. Nailing a challenging performance while helping to bring a story to life must be very fulfilling. And signing autographs must feel very cool.

I've wondered what it would be like to attend the Oscars. All dressed up, rubbing elbows with legends. I've imagined what it would be like to win an Oscar—and not just any Oscar, but the one for Best Actor. What a feeling of surprise and delight a person must feel as they stand up from their seat to take the stage, where they get to say something insightful and memorable in the presence of all their peers, competitors and critics.

What could be better than that?

I'll tell you what's better than that: Best Actor/Actress *in a Supporting Role*.

A quick look at the names of winners in these categories illustrates what I'm saying: Ingrid Bergman, Frank Sinatra, Meryl Streep, Morgan Freeman, Jack Lemmon, Judi Dench, Robert De Niro, Mahershala Ali, Robin Williams, Octavia Spencer, Denzel Washington, Jamie Lee Curtis, Brad Pitt.

No doubt you know these names, because they're legends. There's a magical potency in their performances and in the roles they play—particularly when they're in scenes with the lead characters. We wouldn't get to know the protagonists nearly as well without the foil supplied by these secondary roles. They build on and develop the main character by reflecting back to them their motives, desires and weaknesses.

Choosing to be a supporting actor makes a quiet statement, too, but a strong one: You're so good at what you do that you have nothing to prove. The roles you accept now are the ones that have the potential to make other people shine.

The world knows you're a star. *We* know that *you* know you're a star. But are you that rare kind of star that guides others to be great?

That's the game we're playing now.

Mentorship is not a status, something you deserve because you've paid your dues. It isn't slick, or smooth, or scripted. It isn't set at the fancy table near the window where people flock so you can share your wisdom, as if mentorship were a one-way knowledge transfer. And time at your elbow doesn't magically grow people like mushrooms under manure.

If any of these ideas motivated you to pick up this book, there's some work to do.

It used to be about you. But it's not this time.

Who's the Leader Here?

In Roy Group's research into the stories people tell about their mentors, one of the strongest themes is the importance of mentors and mentees being recognized by the other party as leaders. Mentees need to acknowledge that mentors have a rich and valuable life experience that they're prepared to share, and mentors must treat their mentees as leaders deserving of interest and respect. They must fully acknowledge the ups and downs of their mentees' experiences—the challenges and struggles they are facing, and the wear and tear their responsibilities are taking on their lives. If leaders learn most from their own experience (which they do—*all* humans do), then the primary role of mentors is to enhance this learning for their mentees.

This flies in the face of some of the norms surrounding mentorship relationships.

At Roy Group, we encounter many formal mentorship programs where participants often comment on how valuable the mentors are to the initiative, for example:

> These are incredible people with incredible knowledge and experience for you to draw on. Make sure that you read up on the bios provided to you about your mentor and their accomplishments and be prepared for your conversations with them. Their time is valuable; please do not waste this opportunity.

These mentorship programs typically put the spotlight on how generous, knowledgeable and experienced the mentors are. Mentees are encouraged to treat their mentors with respect, and everybody thanks the mentors for their effort.

There's nothing wrong with this in itself—gratitude is one of the most powerful engines in leadership. But this approach to mentorship orients us towards seeing mentors as the leaders in the equation; the mentees are lucky just to follow along. The necessary conclusion about who's most important is heavily skewed.

But we saw something different in our research. Data set after data set showed that if the focus remains on the mentor for too long, it can snuff out the flame of a mutually significant relationship.

Rather than falling all over ourselves to acknowledge mentors, a better way forward is for mentors to acknowledge who they're stepping up for.

They're stepping up for mentees—because what younger generations are leading through is more complex than it's ever been. It's *their* time (that could be spent leading big things). It's *their* experience (that will ultimately shape them). It's how *they* respond (that will determine the kinds of stories that unfold in the world).

Mentorship relationships deepen when the way mentors connect, spend time and tackle things together with their mentees is rooted in the fundamental principle that mentors must help leaders lead their own endeavours. This principle guides how a mentor offers their advice or coaching: They keep their focus on the experience of their mentee, not the value of their own, as remarkable as it may be.

TACTIC **Balancing Attention and Intention**

This is a relatively simple tactic with potentially dramatic implications. It involves noticing how much of any given dialogue—one within yourself, within your mentee or between the two of you—is focused on intention and what needs to happen, and how much is simply paying attention to what *is*.

Cultivating intention includes

- taking actions we could, should or want to take;
- thinking through how we need to address issues; and
- choosing the best way forward from all the current options.

Paying attention includes

- acknowledging physical sensations and emotions related to what needs to be addressed;
- creating space to understand deep motivations and dynamics in the subconscious; and
- reflecting on connections, patterns and underlying themes within an issue.

By helping our mentees pay attention first, in the right proportion, we often make it easier for them to craft the right intentions in due course.

REFLECTION

- Who is the Best Supporting Actor in your life?
- Who are you the Best Supporting Actor to?

MEDITATION
Share Intelligence— Not Niceties

Share intelligence—not niceties.
The mission others are on,
underneath today's event,
is too important not to be informed.
They need to adjust. They want to improve.
They want to raise their infinite game.

Share intelligence—not niceties.
Break the social contract
and say real things and meaningful things.
Praise devoid of details
is like an invitation
without an address or a time.

Share intelligence—not niceties.
As easy as it comes and with the best of intentions
your encouragement does not mean
that they will be encouraged.

Telling them you believe in them
does not stir their own belief.

Share intelligence—not niceties.
Honesty demonstrates that you were noticing.
Observations demonstrate that you were
paying attention.
Opportunities demonstrate what you sense
is now possible.
Specifics demonstrate your investment
in their process of getting better and better.

Share intelligence—not niceties.
Do not provide what evaporates.
Do not tell someone they've "got this"
to shorten the conversation.
Do not tell someone they are ready.
Look them in the eyes and nod when they tell you.

Share intelligence—not niceties.
Providing encouragement is different
than being an encouraging force.
In the dreadful moments
find some powerful and silent way
to let people know you are there with them.

Encouragement Is a Shortcut

Like most shortcuts, it was an ill-chosen route.
WASHINGTON IRVING, "THE DEVIL AND TOM WALKER"

IT FEELS NICE to say nice things—and it feels nice to hear them.

So why the judgy chapter heading?

I want to be clear before I get into this that I'm not advocating for a world without kindness. Cheering for your children when they step onto the soccer pitch: yes. Big hugs and whispers of "It's *so* good to see you" when visiting old friends: love it. Encouraging words penned on a card for a struggling colleague with an offer to help however you can: wonderful. We need as many acts of love, joy and connection as we can muster.

Life is too difficult to not help each other through. And yet we dare ourselves to forget this. We like to talk about what we did, what we built, what we know. The myth of the self-made individual is one deeply ingrained in our collective psyche. Have you ever noticed that the majority of statues we create are of a single person? We like how simple and clear it feels to point out that some people are just great. Sundeep is successful because he's talented. Mairi was promoted because she's a hard worker.

Personal attributes and habits do go a long way in helping a person thrive—but even the most awesome people needed a myriad of important exchanges with other people along the way. They needed friends, partners, neighbours, colleagues and champions. They needed mentors.

When any one of us is indeed successful in isolating ourselves from a community, the story doesn't generally go down a very good road. It's essential that we pan out a little and recognize the power and value of the support behind the slow unfolding of a given individual's genius. This means wrapping our minds around the complex web of invisible light that connects us to one another.

Encouragement is one of these very common community touchpoints—a nudge we often use to interact with others along the journey of life. Encouragement is always at the ready to fill a gap: A peer confides they're feeling overwhelmed by their job and think they might have to quit. Or a friend's son is in the crosshairs of a terrible hockey coach and is considering giving up and going home. Our first response is often empathy—we can easily conjure how that must feel, and we know it's not good. We want that person to know we believe they're capable of working through the uncomfortable situation they're facing, and so we hear ourselves saying something to convey that they've "got this," that we believe in them and that it's all going to work out.

We encourage because it allows us to express what we would like to see happen. It feels like a little shortcut from where the person in front of us is today to an ideal state we'd like to see them reach.

I believe there's something more valuable we can do for others in these moments. I'm asking mentors to cultivate a careful and conscious relationship with encouragement and not take this shortcut. I'm asking them to tap into their empathy, but rather than expressing it as simple encouragement, to decode it and channel it into what's most helpful.

Do I want people to be heartened by interactions with their mentors? Yes. Do I want people to move forward with clarity, calm and capability? Yes. Do I think this is best accomplished by a mentor providing encouragement? No.

Choices in the Cockpit

In chapter 5, I introduced the primacy of conduct. How I choose to conduct myself creates an atmosphere inside other people, and they make this atmosphere mean something about themselves. Our ability to influence others—and what they're capable of creating—begins with this dynamic.

When I think about conduct and all the options I might access in a given situation, the number is staggering. I could pay close attention to a person, or squander that attention on any number of internal or external distractions. I could choose to share advice or share a story. I could raise my voice or an eyebrow, make a face or flip a sarcastic thumbs-up. So many options.

At any given moment, I may be drawing on several options and wrapping them all into how I behave. When we just wing it, instead of taking a breath to centre ourselves, our conduct can become a bit like a dirty snowball on the playground that's made up of all kinds of ingredients—some of which might cause unintentional harm when thrown someone else's way.

Whenever I'm being conscious about the way I'm conducting myself, I find myself drawing on the metaphor of being a seaplane pilot: on my own, keenly aware that I am high above the ocean and within short reach of all kinds of levers, dials and knobs spread across every square inch of the console. This gives me a wide array of adjustment options to support or steer what's unfolding around me and make my way to where I'm trying to get to.

With every intentional choice we make with these controls, we shape our journey, taking 100 percent responsibility for how we respond to the elements around us.

Imagine a lever in the middle of the console that moves horizontally, and its two ends are labelled "Encouragement" and "Information." All the many combinations of encouragement and information are spread between these two poles along a spectrum. There's probably some dust on this lever; we don't often adjust it from the default position we typically keep it in. For many of us, its position is much closer to Encouragement than Information.

We don't even really think about the way we provide encouragement. It just tumbles out of us.

You likely have a way of providing encouragement to others that feels natural, even automatic. I'd like to ask you to suspend this default setting. Step back and reflect on how your approach has been influenced by the way encouragement showed up in your family and in the places you grew up.

In the town where I grew up, many adults were quick to say something like, "Great job today." They always did it in a friendly but passing way. After the mini-hit of nice, these interactions always left me curious. *What had I done that they noticed most? What aspects of what I was doing had I got right? What did they think the next step could be?* These very pleasant adults in my world had acknowledged me, but they also sent the message that they were on their way to something else and didn't have time to discuss what I'd done beyond dropping a few words of praise.

These people worked hard and were relatively friendly, but they also had a way of keeping their cards close to their chest. It was just our prairie way. Encouragement was something shared in passing, the same way that "Hey, how's it going?" was a common way to say hello. An answer was rarely expected, or even possible, in the few available seconds. It was never really a question, even though your neighbour wanted to know that everything was okay for you. You had to decode their greeting, and what it really meant was a very genuine "I hope everything's going great for you."

Moments of encouragement, both when we receive it or we default to providing it, connect us to a thousand tiny pieces of nostalgia like this: those moments when adults noticed us and affirmed us . . . or could have, and failed to.

We don't even really think about the way we provide encouragement. It just tumbles out of us. If we can begin to recognize this—and understand that just because something feels automatic doesn't mean it's the sweet spot—we may find an even sweeter spot. One that creates more positive impact and more reason for others to believe in themselves. We may be able to find a setting that's more helpful. For mentors, a conscious approach to how they deploy encouragement can make a big difference.

The Unintended Consequences of Encouragement

We offer up encouragement naturally and it spills from us effortlessly to break an awkward moment. But there's not just one downside to encouragement—there are four. They don't make it bad or wrong, just less helpful than something else could have been.

First, encouragement often fills a void with something that's pleasant but not entirely healthy—a bit like cotton candy rather than quinoa. It's fun, it's nice and sweet, but it's just not very nutritious. We offer it to take the sting out, to let someone know we support them and to keep them going. But after a nice little sugar high, what we said hasn't provided what they need to move forward.

Second, encouragement can be an unintentional distraction. Let's say I'm throwing a baseball with my niece, Charley, in the backyard. The joy of play takes us both over. We stop thinking about what we need to do to catch the ball; it just happens. Our focus follows the ball back and forth, and is rewarded by the satisfying slaps into our glove pockets. Even the sting in our palm is fun: a sharp little signal confirming every catch. We start throwing harder because it feels good to send the ball to the other person with some heat on it. Subtle smiles of mischief connect us in an exchange that's much richer than just playing catch.

In all of this, it becomes easy for me to slip into "uncle mode"—the unconscious habit of saying "good catch" every time she makes one. Without even realizing it, I've set myself up for an unintended dynamic: When she eventually misses a catch, it feels like the best option I have is saying nothing. But the effect of that isn't neutral. The space left by my lack of encouragement now fills my niece's head with doubt and distraction, and she wonders if she's let me down somehow. She'd picked up the ball and turned to read my face for a message, and didn't get one. Am I disappointed in her? Am I even having a good time?

I would have been a better partner if I had withheld the running commentary and focused the entire time, allowing each of us to drop into flow and enjoy this time together without distraction and without wavering amidst all the catches and misses.

The third unintended consequence of encouragement is that it can create a false sense of readiness. As mentors, our hopeful confirmation that someone has "got this" carries significant weight. We offer it as encouragement, but it's received as an assessment. What's more important and valuable is for us to help the person in front of us assess their own situational awareness, including any areas of doubt that need attention.

Lastly, when encouragement is overused as a tactic to urge people forward, it can compromise our credibility. We all have someone in our lives who over-encourages. Praise is the daily special and boundless positivity is on tap. It's automatic for them; they can hardly stop themselves from providing it. They express how highly they think of us, how much they believe in us and how they know we could do anything. We expect this from them and come to count on it. But over time, we become desensitized to this unconditional optimism, and what they say loses its meaning. We finally get our fill of the cotton candy.

Society's "encouragement default" is still expanding, too. Think back to when you witnessed your first standing ovation as a young person. It signalled a very special emotional resonance, right? Brought on by a performance's potency? A standing ovation was hard-won, and precious.

Now think about how they happen more often nowadays. If we give a standing ovation to every impressive performance, how do we signal our appreciation to those artists who create truly rare and exceptional experience?

Shifting Towards Information

So what would be more helpful and more discerning than defaulting to encouragement?

It's as easy as moving that lever in front of us in the direction of Information.

When a mentee is equipped with relevant and up-to-date intelligence in the form of observations, they have the opportunity to make informed adjustments to their approach while retaining ownership of the challenge at hand. They self-correct their way to the outcome they're trying to create. When we find the clearest way possible to provide someone else with information, they don't have to analyze, argue or even think about it. They simply adjust according to what they now know about a situation and what's required by it. Better yet, the information doesn't always need to come from the mentor. With the right kind of mentor on the scene, the best set of information can come from the mentee's own reflection on their experience.

Let's look at the power of the subtle difference between encouragement and information in an organizational context.

It's a given that leaders are encouraged to celebrate the successes of others. When your team sees a challenging project through, you might order pizza and beer, and throw a few work hours into revelling in the win. This is the equivalent of encouragement, if you leave it at that celebration state. A pizza party says, "We did good!"

Yet right there lies an opportunity for something much more powerful.

With that tasty pizza in one hand and a cold beer in the other, all you need to do is be the kind of leader who quietly converts the celebration into a conversation:

"Could we take a moment to talk about all the factors that went into this success?"

The conversation that follows will pay for the pizza and beer a thousand times over.

The best leaders do the same thing with wipeouts. When their team fails and a project goes off the rails, the first thing they do is order food. And with the same tone in their voice—and the same look on their face—they make a toast to those challenges that kick our asses and ask, "Could we take some time to talk about all the factors that conspired to trip us up?"

Out comes the intel.

Who knew? Failure as an information source is as nutritious as anything for deepening ownership, encouraging self-correction and ultimately succeeding.

Let's dig deeper into the idea of emotion as a source of information, too. Strong emotion in the other person tends to paralyze us in

No shortcut that we provide, however well-meaning, can compare to someone lighting their own fire from within.

an interaction, perhaps because it taps a deep respect for the fact that the person in front of us is going through something big. This "oh shit!" reaction creates a vacuum that we're then seriously tempted to fill with something nice to say, or something that tells the person we're on their side.

Someone tears up in frustration with their business partner. Or pounds the table with a fist to express that they've had it with their team's low level of passion. Or breaks down because this is the second time in a row they haven't been able to make payroll.

These are the moments that beg us to say something comforting—to wish the emotion away. But we also have the opportunity to wring the emotion, whatever it is, for the information it holds. Rather than saying, "Oh wow, you really need to talk to them about this," or "So frustrating. I know exactly how you feel," recognize that you have the opportunity to find out more.

"I can see this is really hurting you. What about all this is the sharpest edge?"

Or, "What are they doing that tells you they don't care?"

Out comes the intel again. For your mentee, having someone who shows up steady, solid and interested in them, while also acknowledging the mentee's emotion, will almost always allow them to describe why the emotion exists rather than being gripped by it.

Helping people review their own experience, alongside our observations about specific aspects of their performance, provides them with a fuller perspective on what is real, what's available to them and what is now possible moving forward. This invites a motivation to adjust and move forward again. The experience remains theirs to engage and theirs to win. No shortcut that we provide, however well-meaning, can compare to someone lighting their own fire from within.

Say your mentee is nervous about their upcoming pitch to potential funders. Rather than telling them they've "got this," it's more helpful to outline the evidence behind your conviction: "I need to remind you that you often get nervous before presentations—but then you connect with everyone in the room with your sincerity and obvious preparation. In the past, we've spoken about how caring about projects being done well is why you put yourself under pressure to perform. It sounds like that's happening again."

Rather than simply saying, "I believe in you" to our children, how about demonstrating that belief by putting them in charge of something important to the family? Organizing the family vacation. Creating a design for the garden. The message is clear—and it never even had to cross your lips.

Rather than saying, "Everything will work out—it always does" to our colleague who's struggling, we might serve them better by saying, "I sense this is really tiring you out. Would it help to go for lunch and talk about it?"

Demonstrating your belief that someone is capable and committed to improving is even more encouraging than encouragement itself.

TACTIC Converting Encouragement to Information

This is a very subtle shift that takes some private effort and focus to start doing habitually. Once you start replacing encouragement with information, you will find that your mentee experiences much more long-lasting and self-sustaining motivation—the original purpose of your encouragement.

The key is to notice. Notice which encouraging words you would like to share. For example: "Don't give up. You can do it."

Then notice where the desire to encourage comes from, which might be any of:

1. I want this person to keep going; I sense a breakthrough moment is near.
2. I want to be seen as friendly.
3. I want to be seen as this person's champion.

Now notice which of these desires is helpful. Usually it will be number 1. Numbers 2 and 3 are often not helpful and can be set aside.

Here are some other questions to consider, with sample responses:

How would I like the other person to feel after I share what I'm about to say?

"A renewed sense that persevering might have a reward."

What would I like them to be capable of?

"Sticking it out to get to a new chapter of their work."

What specific instances or patterns in the past come to mind?

"When they competed hard to get this current role."

What evidence exists within these moments that the person is capable of this?

"The future was unclear, yet you set your mind to it and saw it through."

How would I like to share the evidence I have that they're capable?

"I remember so clearly when you competed for this role. It seemed unlikely to go your way but you set your mind to it and saw it through. This situation reminds me of that."

REFLECTION

- Who is the most encouraging person in your life?
- What is it that they most specifically recognize in you?

MEDITATION
Questions Set Us Free

―――――――――

Questions set us free.
Drawing on the black and white of all we know.
Tapping into the splashed colours of all we can imagine.
Crafted in the moment
from every stolen glimpse
and overheard whisper.

Questions set us free.
Collaborating like operators
to re-find our futures.
Allowing us to piece together
that which does not yet exist
and to experience how good it feels already.

Questions set us free.
Inviting us to take stock of what is
and what we have made that mean.
Tasking us to inventory
the dynamics that will make this easy
and the nuances that will make this hard.

Questions set us free.
Flying low over multiple routes
to assess which way feels best.
Sifting through what we thought was true
and separating what we need
from all the things we thought we wanted.

Questions set us free.
Eliciting courage and candour, creativity
and promises at the boundary
of what we know and what we don't
so that we can advance.
They take us to the other side.

Questions set us free.
They establish rapport with our captors.
They case the joint.
They identify the secret rendezvous point.
They expose the possibility
and whisper for us to go.

12

You Are Not Asking Enough Questions

Live the questions now. Perhaps you will then, gradually, without noticing it, live your way into the answer some distant day.

RAINER MARIA RILKE, IN A LETTER TO HIS PROTÉGÉ, FRANZ XAVER KAPPUS

THINK OF your favourite dinner guest. The person you invite back again and again. At the end of the night when you say goodbye, the way you feel prompts you to dream up the next time you can invite this person over.

Now think about some of the mentors you've had in your life. The people you sought out when you needed support, counsel or maybe a good kick in the pants. A person you called on the holidays to find out how they were, and after hanging up the phone you realized they had once again turned the conversation back to being about you and how you were doing.

What do these people have in common? They are curious, attentive, patient, confident and able to take a conversation wherever it needs to go. And they enjoy time with you. They don't judge where the conversation goes, though they will steer it from time to time. They take everything that's going on around them and craft it into another question.

Mentorship is fuelled by questions.

I introduced inquiry in chapter 4 as one of the four key disciplines a mentor must practise, and invite the leaders they're working with to practise with them.

Questions, and our ability to craft them, are key. Well-crafted questions create connection and engagement. They send a message straight to someone's heart that we believe they are intelligent and capable and resourceful. Questions place our focus on what's most important: the real experience of the person with the responsibility to take something forward. Before we find out what instruction is needed or share a single piece of advice, questions help us uncover the context of what *is*.

If questions invite people in, an absence of questions repels them. Unintentionally, it sends a message to people that we believe we are more intelligent, capable and resourceful than they are. And this gets in the way of our ability to connect the way we want to.

I'm often approached by someone who wants to earn the word *mentor*, and who by every measure should be a shoo-in. They're accomplished and generous, with lots of knowledge to transfer and insights to share.

I'll ask them to tell me about the kinds of questions they're asking. That's when many people realize they're not asking enough questions—or any at all.

The simple shift for would-be mentors is to tap into that same place inside where all the opinions and value-adds are coming from and rummage around until they can find some curiosity, some interest and some acknowledgement of the people they're talking to.

Becoming a mentor cannot happen unless you are curious—genuinely curious—about the experience, state, gifts and endeavours of other people.

But can we really rely on questions to be the foundation of our relationship with those who are looking to us for mentorship? My answer to that is yes. Questions help us understand what instruction and knowledge transfer are required. Questions help us discern what advice is actually valuable. Questions can be fun, interesting and enlightening. Questions can also be rigorous and cut to the core of what's getting in the way.

The Power of the Little Claw

There's another reason why questions, and our ability to carefully and methodically craft them, are important. We don't commit to curiosity this way just to be a nice or generous person, or to get invited back for dinner. We do it to create a deep sense of ownership where it belongs: inside the people we're talking with. Whether in a one-on-one or a group setting, questions allow the people in front of us to pull apart their current (usually limited) thinking and create some space within it, helping them understand what their situation is really about and what it represents. It allows them to articulate what something more ideal would look like and stirs the desire to start moving in that direction. The act of responding not only helps people craft a plan informed by both conscious and unconscious awareness of their situation, it encourages people to prepare themselves to start making it happen.

Questions allow others to take ownership of their experience, and responsibility for how they've contributed to the current situation. They allow people to take stock of what that situation is, both on the surface and in all the layers of meaning and emotion beneath it. And questions help them to strategize different ways forward. The better the questions, the more ownership responding creates.

Great questions allow the other person to fully grasp what's required of them as a leader.

What any of us wants most from a mentor is someone who is focused on our experience as a leader, not theirs as a mentor. When mentorship relationships last, the person on the receiving end feels the full ownership, responsibility and even pressure that come with their role.

This is another paradox. By being with someone in a certain way—accompanying them with a measure of self-discipline and restraint—we help them decipher what they alone must take accountability for. By concentrating more on our being—and less on what we know and do—we help another person know, do and be more.

This may be best expressed in the form of a personal story.

When Questions Aren't Messing Around

As a young CEO in Scotland, I had a serious weakness: finance. My brain was drawn to ideas, not figures. When asked about financial matters, I would always spin a little and then pass things off to someone else in the room. I felt like financial constraints got in the way of creativity. I was young and had lots of energy. But rather than hiring someone else, I was happy to invest my own elbow grease.

I'd worked my way through my first job in New York as an experience creator and a program person. Most of what I had created was with shoestring budgets, and a lot of heart and discretionary effort from my teams. We could make a lot happen for a group of participants just by being there, together. We didn't make much money as a division—or lose any. It almost felt like we were a band doing gigs and having fun on tour.

Our creations landed me my first big leadership assignment at Columba. Somewhere deep down, my belief persisted that if we worked as hard as we could, we'd be all right.

It was obvious that this belief shone through in my early reports to the board (not in a good way). After one meeting a few months in, one of the board members, Liz McAreavey, came to me with an offer I couldn't refuse.

"You should spend a day with my husband, John," she said. She felt I could learn a lot from him. I thought it sounded like a great idea.

Her husband was an accountant, and *her* accountant—a formidable ace up her sleeve when it came to getting entrepreneurial ventures off the ground.

I showed up at their home for an 8 a.m. start on a Saturday morning, having no idea that this day was going to change the course of the enterprise I was in charge of.

John's office was a huge room lined by books on three walls and floor-to-ceiling windows on the fourth. In the centre stood a small,

Great questions allow the other person to fully grasp what's required of them as a leader.

———————

elegant writing desk with a laptop, one chair facing the computer and a second chair on the side of the desk. That second chair was for me.

John was a no-nonsense sort of guy. It was exciting to be near him because of his focus more than anything else. I would find out in the hours ahead that John did not miss a thing.

He went into a mode, one that involved crafting a question and then listening carefully to each and every answer. Every once in a while, he'd take a moment to adjust or enter data into the spreadsheet he was creating as we spoke. He asked me questions about the concept of our enterprise: what we were all about and why we were doing what we did. He asked me why I'd moved across an ocean with a young family to take the job. He asked me what I wanted our brand to be about. He asked who our work was most valuable to. He asked about revenue. He asked how we used time to create revenue. And he asked me about expenses. If I didn't know something, he didn't even look up from the laptop to say, "Can you please phone someone who does know?"

We didn't break for coffee. We didn't break for lunch. He asked me questions for five hours.

Then he asked if I would go away for a few hours. Maybe get something to eat. Which sounded like a really great idea because I was a little dizzy from the morning's interrogation.

When I came back, it was like a new assignment. John had shifted into a different mode—information sharing.

"I have good news and then bad news," he said. "The good news is here in the bottom right-hand corner of this spreadsheet. This is a projected annual return that your team could attain. With three years left in your contract, that means you could leave three times that much in the coffers for the next CEO and the next chapter of the organization."

His clarity broke me like a twig. Tears welled up in my eyes. To actually see those numbers and know that this could happen brought a strange mix of relief, a hunger to achieve and embarrassment—up till then I'd been sustaining myself with a blind trust that it would all work out. But now I had a blueprint. All I had to do was find a way to make each one of those little digital boxes real.

"So the bad news is this," he said next, a sobering cue to snort back my tears and listen up. "You're missing a piece."

"What piece is that?" I wanted that missing piece bad, whatever it was.

"I don't know what the piece is, but it has a few features," he said. "It has all the magic that your current programs have, it just needs to be worth more." He told me how much profit this missing piece needed to create and a guess at what the program in total would need to be sold at. "I've marked six areas in these blue cells across the year's forecasts, which are the months where this program needs to happen. You need to do it six times a year.

"Without this piece," he continued, "it looks like this." He zeroed the six blue boxes. That heartening sum in the bottom right-hand corner went sub-zero instantly. So did the temperature of my spinal fluid. "But, again, this is what it looks like *with* the piece." He put the numbers back in the six blue boxes. "And that brings your annual return back."

Anyone who's financially minded will know what John was actually telling me: If we continued to work the way we were working, going down the path I was leading us down, we would have gone broke. But rather than telling me that, he framed it all as a challenge. All I had to do to make this enterprise whole, as a CEO, was to go out into the world and find that missing piece.

"Do you have any idea what the piece is?" I asked as I pulled on my boots and got ready to drive home.

"You're the experience guy, Chiz. You'll find it. Or you'll create it."

Which we did.

The power of that comprehensive analysis of our situation, created through John's questions, had provided me with a clear focus. My team lived the question with me until we started living the answer.

Within ten days, an opportunity presented itself in the form of a remarkable partner and a brilliant idea. It was a new concept pitched to a new market, one that would allow us to charge a premium—more than even John had recommended—by doing something that no one else could do.

The Gemini Project was a leadership development initiative pairing ten young people from difficult socio-economic realities in Glasgow with ten senior and/or emerging leaders from financial institutions in Edinburgh. We didn't do it six times a year, we did it ten times a year. We became the *it* program for developing "leadership beyond title." And this incredible piece that was no longer missing—and the stir it created—brought us to the doorstep of our next game-changing opportunity.

None of this would have happened without my day with John. His ability to craft questions that unearthed all the information I needed, paired with his ability to then organize that information, made me hungry to go and accomplish what I was responsible for.

Your Brain on Questions

In reflecting on this story, what's most interesting to me is that mode John went into for those first hours, looking across the desk at me—someone he'd just met—and committing in that way to help me clearly understand the challenge I faced. He didn't take the challenge away from me or try to sort it himself. He just wanted to get my head in the game.

In those moments, his brain pulled out all the stops. He dived below the concept I was carrying around in my head. He was mapping out the complete context. To do this, he drew on his ability to understand something new, and imagined with me what "good" needed to look like. He was recognizing patterns in what I said to identify where he was going to have to dig deeper. He was creating a new pattern that financially was more cogent. He was discerning anything that could be converted into currency. He scanned my descriptions for gaps, crafting questions to make sure we filled them in. He was converting the conceptual into the practical. All in real time.

I've had clients in the early stages of their coaching practice describe their brain as something akin to a two-tier workshop when they're crafting questions. They listen carefully to their client downstairs near the cash register, then have to climb a ladder to the workshop area to find the next question they want to use. Once they have a question 80 percent ready, they slide down the ladder and use it. They listen again. Up and down. They use all of their brain to take the conversation where it needs to go next.

TACTIC **Opening Up Closed Questions**

Lawyers are rigorously conditioned to only ask a question in court when they know what the answer will be. This allows them to create a line of questioning that takes a case towards a preferred conclusion—like a train that will get them to their destination. Mentors need to be the opposite of this. They need to ask the kinds of questions that might send them in any number of different directions (which is a job for a helicopter, as I'll discuss in the next chapter).

Any time the question we ask can be answered with a yes or no, it is called a closed question. Closed questions can be useful to plant a flag in the sand to mark a clear decision in the conversation. For example:

- Are you prepared to take this on?
- Are you willing to give this person another chance?
- In your heart of hearts, have you already made a decision about this?

You can see how a closed question can establish clarity and save some time in the conversation. My only warning is that I've learned to not believe everything people say. It's not that they're lying to you, it's just that they think they've given you their final answer—and they may simply need you to confirm that a little later, just in case there's been a shift. Sometimes people need to say something out loud to begin the process of finding out it isn't true.

Open questions, on the other hand, get us lots of information. Oftentimes we can take what starts in our mind as a closed question and open it up:

- In what ways do you feel prepared to take this on?
- In what ways do you not feel prepared?
- What makes you want to give this person another chance?

- What makes you not want to?
- How close are you to making a decision about this?

TACTIC **Requesting Self-Crafted Questions**

When we ask questions as mentors, our brain shifts into the inquiry mode that John was in. So why wouldn't we share that mode with the people we're working with?

There have been several moments when I've been in the mentor's chair and honestly had no idea of where the conversation needed to go next. So I had to ask the party in front of me for help:

- Where does our conversation need to go from here?
- What is the most valuable question I could ask you right now?
- What is the most important question I could ask you in this conversation?
- What is the toughest question I could ask you about this?

These moments when we decide to be transparent about not knowing are golden opportunities. The other person will often stop in their tracks and shift into question mode. Their brain will take stock of everything that has been said—and what hasn't been said, since they have access to that, too. They won't worry about what the answers will be; our brains can't do these two things at once. They will craft themselves a question. And it will be a good one.

All we have to do is ask them their question. This can be done in the moment, or in advance of a conversation. Often I will send an email ahead of time together with a client and request a cluster of five to ten questions that they are keen to dig into, or know they need to dig into. Sometimes there's a pattern to the questions they provide that's worth discussing before we get into the questions themselves. Sometimes it makes sense for us to change the order of the questions. Sometimes I might add supplemental questions as we go. And sometimes I just stick with the script of questions they've provided.

Self-crafted questions are a wonderful way to steer the conversation towards the heart of the matter. They're also a great way of creating a perfect balance of safety and risk. There's no real way I can take offence to the intimacy of a question my mentor asks when I'm the one who crafted the question.

TACTIC **Adopting Emergent Questions**
There are times when we don't even have to ask someone to craft their own question. They just throw one out. These are often questions that come from a place of strong emotion, so handle their question with care and wait for the right moment to bring their attention to it:

- (Joy) How could I have been so lucky for this to be happening?
- (Frustration) What do they even expect from me in a situation like this?
- (Confusion) What am I supposed to do now?

The tactic with these is a pretty easy one. Take that question (that people don't even realize was a question because it was just what came out of their mouth), clean up the dish it came on and set it on the table down in front of them:

- What makes you feel lucky about what is happening?
- What are the expectations you have to meet in this situation?
- What do you feel able to do to respond to this?

The reason they asked the question they did is because they wanted to answer it.

REFLECTION

- What are ten things you would like to know about other people (each in the form of a question)?
- What is your own answer to each of these questions?

MEDITATION
Time to Move

―――――――――

Time to move.
Airborne perspective provides
a heightened capability
to discern the unique challenge
presented by the territory
being accessed.

Time to move.
Releasing ourselves
from the muck and mire.
Sorties to where we need,
would like and would love
to be.

Time to move.
Restlessly and carefully hovering
above what is.
Looking down and taking stock
of the forces at play
in the current state of affairs.

Time to move.
Gathering fragments of what's possible.
Wandering wide outside
the obvious, the tried, the true.
Daring each other
to be wild in what we could do.

Time to move.
The path is not clear
but in the right direction,
and with resources along the way.
We have enough to make
our advance.

Time to move.
Paying close attention
to each broken twig,
to each dead end,
to each milestone,
to each glimpse and whisper.

13

Strategy on the Fly

*Our task is not to put the greatness back into humanity,
but to elicit it, for the greatness is there already.*
**JOHN BUCHAN (LORD TWEEDSMUIR),
FIFTEENTH GOVERNOR GENERAL OF CANADA**

A MENTOR ONCE told me that a question is our only connection to the future. Otherwise the future doesn't exist; it is something that humankind assumes is real. He said that it's by asking questions that we help each other to re-find that elusive future again and again—and increase our chance to bring it into being.

To me a good question feels like throwing a single pebble into a lake, as opposed to a handful of gravel. Then I throw the next pebble, and the next. My best questions always use as few words as possible and constitute clear requests for interesting information.

But how do you choose which pebble to toss next?

Let's imagine you are with a fine young leader who's just been handed a sensitive file. They're trying to wrap their head around the situation and how they'll address it. They feel the responsibility but just don't know what to do. It's the conversation before the moment of performance, and you're conscious that the finest thing you can do right now is to calmly and methodically craft some questions to get all the information out on the table.

This information will come in a lot of forms. There might be some numbers and metrics. There might be examples of success. And of failure. There might be emotions and weak, non-verbal signals of all kinds. It's all important. And you get it out by asking questions.

I don't want this chapter to leave you with the message that you need to ask more questions without providing you with ways of practising. But that requires a model, which I've always been wary of using. It's hard to imagine a model that doesn't miss something or somehow stifle the conversation. I don't like feeling handcuffed by models or distracted by them, and sometimes I set them aside. But occasionally there's a model that's incredibly helpful in focusing our efforts and navigating a situation with some method.

HELI is both an acronym (which I'll detail shortly) and a metaphor (of a helicopter). As a model, this makes it easy to recall in the moment and simple to use.

A good HELI conversation feels like a helicopter ride:

- Safety is the primary priority—but there may be some uncomfortable bumps.
- If we do hit some bumps, we're going to remain steady and focused.
- Time in a helicopter is valuable, so we use it with clear intent.
- We need to concentrate: Distractions must be managed down towards zero.
- We have almost limitless options for where we can go.
- Agility, the ability to move in any direction we need to, is a key advantage.

Once we've checked in with each other on just how important this time is, we can climb on in, fire up this bird and lift up into the sky.

Strategy on the Fly 193

INITIATIVE

Designing and committing to right action.

Converging on clear choices.

Tapping concentrated sources.

Inviting accountability and integrity.

HORIZON

Futuring specific time horizons.

Using senses and emotion to amplify.

Experiencing measurable change in preferred state.

Re-finding what is wanted and why.

LATITUDE

Creating ideas and solution fragments.

Generating divergent possibilities.

Inviting innovative and alternative thought patterns.

Playing with exaggerated constraints and non-constraints.

EXISTENTIAL SCAN

Taking inventory of resources.

Sensing forces at play in current state.

Identifying dynamics for and against.

Creating an overview of what is and what meaning has been made.

Time Horizons (H)

Sometimes we'll describe a person as visionary—or not. It's the same way we say that someone is creative or not (often about ourselves). The truth is, we all need some support and challenge to be visionary, to be courageous, to be honest with ourselves, to be creative and to keep our word.

The *H* in HELI refers to the *horizon*. It's where we take a reconnaissance with leaders into the future to see what potential is out there.

It might be a short or distant recce into the future:

- What do you need from our conversation an hour from now?
- What would you like to see happen by the end of the day?
- What results would you love to see by the end of the quarter?
- Where would you like your team to be by the end of the year?
- How would you like to experience yourself three years from today?
- What will your enterprise be known for a decade from now?
- What do you see happening in this community one hundred years from now?
- What is most important to protect for the next several generations?

What's important is to find meaningful time horizons that are worth focusing on. Sometimes a leader will mention these as they're talking. We might have to ask questions that help to discern them:

- How long do you think it might take to change this?
- When would be the ideal time for this to be sorted out?
- When will this story start to have an impact that others will experience?

Questions like these allow us to make a decision on where we would like to touch down and explore the future with them. This means landing the helicopter in a selected future scenario, turning the rotors off and getting out to look around. Our language shifts to assessing the environment as if we were there: *What do we see here?* rather than *What would we see there?*

We might go to a future that the mentee *needs* to experience. Or a future we would *like* them to experience. It might be useful for us to travel to the future that unfolds if we just let the status quo take its course. Sometimes, it's very valuable to travel to a future we dread, look it in the face and experience just how much we want to avoid bringing others to this place. The great thing about a helicopter is that it's possible to take recces to several (maybe all) of these time horizons in a single conversation.

In each case, it's important that our questions allow the leaders we're working with to sense that future state as if it were very real:

What do you see around you here?

What do you sense inside you here?

The more we can help a mentee take that critical field trip to the future, the more they will want to accomplish it—or avoid it. It's important to remember this isn't just an exercise in vision, but also motivation. Our brain is motivated by what it sees and senses more than by language alone. Our hunger to make something happen, or avoid it, is amplified when we can imagine what it'll be like when we're actually there. (As an example, my imagined experience of opening the first box of books delivered to my office is the moment that kept me writing this book for almost three years!)

Some things are just easier to talk about when we're in the future. It's easier to articulate what we want and why. It's easier to recognize the strengths that brought us here. To understand the kind of team culture required to sustain us all the way to a place like this. To see what levels and measurable readings are possible here. All we have to do before the helicopter lifts off again is capture as many observations and sensations of this place as we can.

Existential Scan (E)

E stands for *existential scan*. At any time in our conversations, we can always come back to where we started from. We don't have to land back down in the weeds; helicopters have the ability to hover above.

They also have windows by your feet so you can look directly down, notice what's present and take honest stock of what's below you.

In the same way that our mentees need us to help them be visionary, they also need help being honest (mostly with themselves) in their assessment of their current state. This requires a steady hand on the controls and using our conduct to send a clear message: "You can share good news with me right now, and you can share bad news. It's all important information for us to have on the table." The more we can be curious and non-judgmental about what is being shared, the safer it becomes for people to reveal what's really going on with them.

The word *exist* is one to remember here:

- What exists in the here and now?
- What do you notice happening?
- What are the resources available to you?
- What is the state of the relationships around you?
- What are dynamics that will make moving forward easy?
- What are dynamics that will make moving forward difficult?
- What is missing in this situation?
- What's getting in the way?

The related word *existential* reminds us to ask about forces beneath the surface:

- What have others made this mean?
- What stories are being told about this situation?
- What have you made this mean?
- What have you made this mean about yourself?
- What's at stake for you in this?
- What's your appetite to take this on?
- What is this really about?

It's important for mentors to understand that finding out what's really going on involves an honest assessment of external and internal dynamics. For the person we're working with, both are real. Together, they represent the place where all of our progress will start from.

Latitude (L)

Helicopters are versatile and agile. So are leaders who take the opportunity to consider a number of ways forward that "just might work." *Latitude* allows us to see our options from a number of different vantage points relatively quickly, and to explore all the possible ways to get to where we want to go. In exploring *latitude*, leaders need our help to consider a divergent set of alternatives. We don't need them to land on any one way forward here. The leaders we are working with just need to keep considering what might be possible if they use different approaches:

- What would be a bold way to approach this?
- What would be a careful way to approach this?
- Who is someone who would ace this? What would they tell you to do?
- If you knew exactly what to do, what would that be?
- What else?

Mentors can invite even more creativity from leaders if they ask questions that change constraints, just to see what else comes out. They aren't attached to or suggesting any of these ideas in this phase of the conversations; they're just taking some time to challenge convention and be innovative in generating alternatives and ideas for solutions:

- What would you do if you had an entire year to sort this out?
- What would you do if you had only one hour to change this?
- What would you do if you had an unlimited budget to address this?
- How would you make this happen if your budget was zero?
- If you could hire anyone to take this on, who would that be? How would they tackle it?

The person in front of you becomes far more coachable if they understand what it is you're trying to help them find.

Creating the space for some *latitude* leads to intuition, creativity and glimpses of what might be possible.

Initiative (I)

Eventually in our conversations, it becomes clear that we've explored enough to make some choices about going forward. Changing conditions may need to be monitored and some level of ambiguity will always be present, but it's time to determine what actions will move us in the right direction. Rather than being creative like we were in *latitude*, now is the time to be a designer—to take *initiative*:

- What is it time for?
- In this particular set of circumstances and constraints, what ways forward might work?
- Which ways are you choosing?
- How will you know if they start to work? How will you know if they start to fail?
- What are your first steps forward?
- Who needs to know about your approach?
- Who can make this easier?
- By when do you need each of these steps to happen?

This is the time to converge on clear choices of where investment of time, money, resources and talent will be made. It's the time to engage with others to share understanding and align.

This is also the time to get leaders to focus, and to make some promises about how they'll get traction moving forward. I use the word *promises* here rather than *commitments* because I find it conveys the nature of adult-to-adult relationships better: We make promises to each other because we choose to, not because we are required to.

TACTIC Deploying the HELI Conversation

When we have an option like the HELI model up our sleeve, we can feel a strange temptation to use it covertly, not telling the other party what we're doing. I think we do this because we like our skill in conversation to seem unique to us, unassisted by any corny models.

I have found it's better to be transparent.

Let the person know you have a method for the conversation that will allow them to think about things more strategically and really work through them. Explain what H, E, L and I stand for, how each territory the conversation visits will be different and how each will *feel* different. The person in front of you becomes far more coachable if they understand what it is you're trying to help them find.

Crafting questions can initially feel like work. Inquiry is a discipline, not necessarily something we're used to doing. It will take practice.

And the best practice is play. In addition to HELI, here are some of my favourite tactics when it comes to playing with questions.

TACTIC **Offering Creative Containers**

Not everyone enjoys a ride in a helicopter. For some leaders, travelling to future time horizons can feel risky. Questions that may come up for them include:

- What if we create a goal that I can't accomplish?
- What if we commit wholeheartedly to the wrong direction?
- What if I get in trouble for even taking this on?

There are all kinds of things that can get in the way of a person wanting to take that helicopter ride to the future. So we might have to help them get out of their own way.

Sometimes it's easier for people to fill a container with their imagination. For example, you may say to them: Imagine there is a magazine article (choose the relevant publication) about this endeavour. It's the cover story. It explains what you accomplished and how you were able to make that happen.

- What is the title of the article?
- What's the image on the cover?
- What are the most important sections of this story?
- What does each section describe?

Imagine that it's your retirement celebration at (insert your favourite venue here). A surprisingly large group of people has gathered to be part of this moment. There's great food and social connection and high regard for you.

- Who are the people who get up to speak? What do they say?
- How does that go down with you?
- Who surprises you by stepping up to the microphone?
- What do they say? How does that go down with you?

Imagine that you and I meet for lunch a year from today (specific date and place). Everything has worked out the way you needed it to.

- How is it going?
- What are you noticing about your team's performance?
- What are you noticing about your team's learning?
- What are you noticing about your team's engagement?
- What are behaviours that you see happening every day now?
- How does it feel to be you heading back to work after our lunch?

Now imagine that you and I meet for lunch in a year, and things have not gone well. You've actually veered towards a worst-case scenario. Go through the previous list of questions with that in mind.

You can imagine how giving people a container for considering the future allows them to more easily travel with you to a time horizon and fill in the details of what they see and sense. You bring a template and they get to fill in the answers.

Sometimes we all need a little help to daydream.

TACTIC **Including a Third Chair**

If it feels like a mentee is stuck and needs someone else's perspective on their situation, rather than taking the (oh so tempting) opportunity to be that source of advice yourself, a mentor can meet this need by identifying who that someone else might be. You can ask:

- Who would you love to talk about this with?
- Who is someone you know who would deal with this exquisitely?
- Who do you wish was in the room with us right now to tackle this?

At this point, pulling up a third chair for this imaginary guest is good theatre. And now we can tap into whatever perspectives and even advice this person might offer:

- What would this person add to your assessment?
- What question would this person ask you?
- If this person had three pieces of advice for you, what would they be?

Conversations like this unfold quickly and take all kinds of twists and turns. You can have a lot of confidence in (and fun with) these tactics. You know they're going to lead somewhere relevant.

Crafting questions can be challenging, particularly because we're not accustomed to using them as much as we could. They come out awkwardly; we wish we could take them back; we hit dead ends. So we must keep practising. I hope that some of these tactics will make that practice more fun.

REFLECTION

- Describe the physical sensation you experience in a great conversation.
- How might you create this for others more often?

MEDITATION
Share What You Noticed—
Not What You Think

Share what you noticed—not what you think.
As they threw their whole heart into the moment
you were nearby—unseen and unnoticed,
witnessing everything they had to give.
Trust that your line of sight
caught glimpses of genius.

Share what you noticed—not what you think.
Take them back to moments when lips quivered,
eyes twitched and voices broke.
Walk them back—frame through frame
and stop the tape to notice together.
This is when something special happened.

Share what you noticed—not what you think.
Do not come to a conclusion about these moments.
Address each the same as all others.
They were not awesome or disastrous.

They just were what they were.
Let them speak for themselves.

Share what you noticed—not what you think.
Share while the moment still blushes their cheeks.
Stow away and run the review.
Create the space for the moments
to have their say
before they dissolve.

Share what you noticed—not what you think.
When someone has given their all
they are dying to know what you saw
and to see and sense it the way you did.
They know what they were able to do from the inside.
They want to know the impact it had.

Share what you noticed—not what you think.
Steady and grounded,
methodical and measured.
Slipping a secret note inside the report
with a message that goes straight to their heart:
"I can't wait to see what you do next."

14

Feedback Helps Us Find Our Way

What you leave behind is not what is engraved in stone monuments, but what is woven into the lives of others.
PERICLES

ONE OF the most powerful strategies mentors have to amplify the performance, learning and engagement of others is to observe them in action carefully and then provide feedback in the form of a debrief or after-action review. When this becomes something leaders can count on from you for its quality, candour and impact, it will transform your relationship, deepen trust and model a way for them to provide this kind of high-quality feedback to others in turn.

Because leaders need feedback. We all need feedback. We always have and always will.

Systems without feedback spin out of control. They become their own kind of monstrous. Relationships in work and personal life go sour when we avoid feedback loops. Community breaks down when there's no mechanism to connect to itself and identify what's really going on. Democracy suffers when feedback loops get distorted and manipulated. Feedback makes a system healthy—and its absence makes a system very ill.

Feedback is a special kind of information drawn from new, real-life experience. It can be focused on anything that a given individual is trying to get better at: making a presentation, convening a conversation, chairing a meeting, working a room.

In addition to the feedback itself, when a mentee is aware that a mentor will provide them with feedback after a performance, they know that someone is invested in them in a real and practical way. They have a partner in giving something their best shot and raising their game for the next time they do it.

Any time we perform a task we're attempting to get better at, we are more focused and more aware of our performance when we know quality feedback is coming. We're open and ready to learn from our own experience. And after we perform, the first thing we want to do is to capture our learning while it's fresh and rich. When mentors become practised in noticing and providing feedback, they become a powerful ally in helping people re-find their potential through continuous learning.

The Kind of Feedback That Changes Things

Feedback is a lot like wine in that quality makes a difference. Mediocre feedback can get the job done, but we may not care too much about hearing it again. (Or it can come with a hangover.) High-quality feedback, by contrast, changes what's possible the moment it's introduced. It enhances everything around it. The giving and receiving of it enhances relationships and even the quality of life.

There are three key factors that mentors need in the feedback they provide. The more they can dare themselves to use these filters in their observations of others and craft their feedback accordingly, the more valuable it will be.

High Specificity

Feedback isn't really feedback unless it's highly specific, and the more so, the better. It may feel zealous, extreme or clinical to provide feedback this way, largely because we aren't used to providing or receiving it at this level of quality.

Highly specific feedback is rare because it takes time, effort and skill to collect and then deliver it. Because of the way most of us have been conditioned, we're not used to dropping into a deep place of noticing without encouraging or intervening.

Feedback is a product of what you saw, heard and maybe even sensed during a given experience. So it's important to take notes to capture your observations with specificity.

High-quality feedback needs to feel like we're reviewing a video of the performance. We should be able to stop the recording at any time to point out the context, actions taken or not taken and any evidence of what impact those actions had. High-quality feedback is about what happened, plain and simple.

Here are some examples of how to enhance specificity when talking to others after an important moment.

Instead of saying, "That's when you asked one of your loaded questions," you could say, "This was the moment you asked Mary 'How long have you been aware of this damage?'"

Or, "I think you asked a question about why she was taking this on" becomes "The conversation changed when you asked your third question, which was 'What is important about this for you?'"

By quoting exact statements word for word, you'll decrease any ambiguity.

If you're reporting the frequency of patterns or occurrences, try specificity instead of judgment:

- "You took up a lot of airspace this morning" becomes "You spoke for a total of twenty-seven minutes in this sixty-minute meeting."
- "You seemed hesitant and a bit unprepared" becomes "Your 'um' count was quite high at forty-two 'ums' in a sixteen-minute presentation."
- "I wondered if there was something wrong with your ear" becomes "I'm not sure you were aware of this, but you were pinching your right earlobe while answering questions."

We take the sting out of generalizing a pattern when we can pay attention and note when and how often it took place: "Then you asked Mary about her awareness of the damage" becomes "At four minutes and thirty-six seconds into the conversation, you asked Mary how long she had been aware of this damage."

Providing an accurate and precise time tag with your observations not only helps the person receiving feedback pinpoint when something happened, but also increases their awareness of how they used their time in general. A specific moment might have occurred earlier or later in the session than they thought. This information will help them use their time more precisely when they next perform.

Highly specific feedback is credible in and of itself. It's hard to argue with or interpret differently. It harnesses the power of observation to provide details that the person within the experience couldn't have noticed on their own. It demonstrates how much focus and attention you brought to what was unfolding. One has to avoid thinking that these statements are hypercritical—they are factual. Whether it is "nice" or not, it is true, and all professionals can benefit from it to perform at their highest level.

Low Judgment

The spirit of feedback is one of investment, not assessment. It's about learning from experience to get better and better. For feedback to work, it needs to be delivered in the language of information—not cheerleading, and not critique.

The model I'll outline in a moment—another that I've found to be robust under all conditions—guides you to use practical and grounded language for classifying three kinds of feedback. I'll take you through them in greater depth, but for now, consider these containers: What worked well? What was tricky? What might be done differently?

Grounded, low-judgment language like this allows people the chance to fully focus on the bullet points of content that come under each heading.

These headings also let you say just about anything you need to say. Coming out of any situation in your life—a stand-up routine at an open mic night, your new CFO's presentation to angry investors, your late-night conversation with customer support—you'll understand there are dynamics that worked well, aspects that were tricky and things that you (or the other party) could do differently next time. There's really nothing else, is there? Fill in these three blanks well, and you'll be providing valuable insights.

Real-Time Offering
Offering feedback in real time is important, but can be difficult to orchestrate in a fast-moving world where one thing is scheduled on top of the next. When your mentee has just thrown their heart into something, they're probably a little tired or dazed. But it's when the experience is fresh that the potential for learning is greatest.

Create an agreement in advance to provide feedback, and build it into your plan. Arrange to go for a coffee after the meeting, or to go through your feedback on the drive home from the presentation. Know what the feedback is going to be focused on in advance and stick to it. Treat the opportunity with some seriousness.

Delivering Feedback Like a Pro
Ritual is an important part of mentorship, and certainly when it comes to delivering feedback. When Roy Group asked our research subjects to identify what made time spent with a mentor valuable, "the repeated use of predictable tools" was a surprisingly popular choice. When people know what's coming next, they can get ready for it. Boring and predictable works. It becomes what people expect. It's tempting to think that as mentors we need to keep things interesting by bringing new conversations to the table. But we don't. Using signature conversational containers over and over again allows their contents to be new, every time, because the situations are always different.

The Feedback Model is one such container. As opposed to the HELI model in the previous chapter, which offers the freedom to take the conversation wherever it needs to go, the Feedback Model is more structured and involves fewer intuitive hunches. Just run this model from top to bottom, filling in the last three sections with the highly specific and low-judgment observations that you collected while watching someone perform.

Your first three questions of a feedback session allow the person who performed to debrief their own performance.

- What worked well?
- What was tricky?
- What might you do differently?

Your next question for them is, "Would you like some feedback from me?"

This question is largely symbolic. Chances are the person you're giving feedback to is going to say yes. But asking is still important, even essential. It creates a contract of agreement that they're up for whatever you have to say. They're agreeing to hear and consider what you noticed. They're saying, "I might take your feedback and build it into what I do next time. I may leave it. But I'm certainly curious to hear what you saw happen."

What follows are your observations and suggested possibilities for improvement:

- What I sensed worked well...
- What I sensed was tricky...
- What I might have done differently...

I will often make a call in advance to discuss how many of each observation I'm hoping to share. Early on in a relationship I might share three key "worked wells," two "trickys" and one exciting "do differently." Over time, I can take these numbers up to whatever's required for a thorough debrief. When I do this right, trust deepens and gives the next opportunity for feedback even more possibilities for candour, insight and risk.

There's no reason to spice the model up. Just focus on loading it with more and more valuable gems. Sometimes creating value means just doing the drill.

One note on the ritual of feedback that I have found very valuable: This model is a very rare example of the power of a one-way

The spirit of feedback is one of investment, not assessment.

---

conversation—twice. The performer has a chance to reflect on their experience, fully and uninterrupted. Then they have a chance to listen to what someone else saw. And then it is over, and the performer makes some choices about how they use this information to self-correct going forward.

If this slides into being a two-way conversation—back and forth after every point—it complicates the transfer of clean perspectives. It becomes a pissing match of reasons why. And it waters down the ritual, reducing the likelihood of another feedback exchange soon.

Nature loves smaller, tighter, more regular feedback cycles. This allows for self-correction that is more precise and more frequent. Feedback often lowers the probability of lurching back and forth between extremes. Feedback makes people excellent.

My Dressing Room Daydream

When we moved back to Canada from the Isle of Skye, there was one daydream sustaining me through the transition. I would now coach one or all of my children in hockey. It was something I started to get excited about before we left Scotland, and once we were back in Canada together, it was just a matter of time before one of them made my dreams come true.

The clearest part of the daydream was using this Feedback Model as a ritual in the dressing room between periods. The time it takes the Zamboni to clean the ice was a perfect window for my dream to happen. I would step into the dressing room with the assistant coaches, a cue to all parents to leave the room. If they weren't going to be on the ice, then they weren't invited to be part of our legendary ritual.

I would ask that room full of seven-year-olds what they thought had worked well.

They would say the darndest things:

"I skated backwards."

"I did crossovers behind the net."

"I got four goals!"

I could see myself being very steady, listening intently and acknowledging every adorable little tidbit they coughed up. And then, with the same look on my face, I'd ask what dynamics had felt tricky. There would be an awkward pause; there almost always is. And then the tidbits would come.

"I was offside for Rhian's breakaway."

"I argued with the referee."

"The reason that Ethan got four goals is that he never passes to anyone else!"

I'd acknowledge those insights with a nod or two, maybe making eye contact with Ethan to let him know I'd be interested in what he had to say next.

After a brief pause, just to make sure we were done (and to let Ethan really hear what was just said), I'd ask what we might do differently in the period ahead.

"I'll focus more on the rush."

"I will be respectful to the referees."

All eyes would turn to Ethan.

"I'll pass the puck more." I think I would wink at Ethan after he said this.

The Zamboni now just a few minutes away from having finished, I'd ask the players if they would like some feedback from me.

They'd say "Yes, Coach!" in unison. (Hey, it's my daydream).

I would pull out a little black notebook and flip to a page with a few bullet points that the assistant coaches and I had talked about during the last period.

I'd make a few specific observations of things we'd seen that seemed to work well. Then I'd note some particular patterns in our team that we sensed were tricky. Then I'd request we do a few things differently.

The siren would sound, and we'd all head back out to the ice. I might discreetly ask Ethan how many passes he was going to try to make this period, and make sure he saw me jot that number down in my book.

And all of that little dream wouldn't have just been making better hockey players. It would have been developing finer young human beings.

That was it. That was my daydream. And I could not wait to start. There was only one problem.

None of my children wanted to play hockey.

I tried everything. Trips to the sports store to look at equipment. Movies about minor hockey. Taking them to games. They tagged along for some time with Dad, but there was never much interest in anything other than the hot chocolate and hot dogs.

What there *was* an interest in was dance. Everyone in my house loves to dance. Around that time my younger son, Oscar, expressed an interest in taking ballet lessons. This was a new world to me and one I knew nothing about. But I was in. If this is what Oscar wanted to do, I would back him 100 percent. I wasn't going to live my dream in that dressing room—but I was excited for him.

Dance recitals are a formidable thing, especially for a rookie dad. They can last for days. There can be what seems like hundreds of performances. There are production crews and video directors, backpacks full of snacks, blister care stations, and racks and racks of costumes. There's tension, rivalry and pressure that's palpable. Dancers, and their parents, are fierce folks.

I watched a lot of dancing. I tried not to look at the program or my watch too often. Some dancers were very good. Some were a bit all over the place. Some *were* all over the place, but so into it that you couldn't help but watch. As much as I thought I was really settling into this new territory of being a dance dad, nothing had prepared me for what would happen next.

The Cricket King

Oscar stepped out onto that stage like he owned it. You could tell he knew it was a full house and that he was dancing for all of us. He was confident and made it look easy and elegant. I think he probably only knew a few basic forms, but you'd have thought he was with the Royal Ballet and just holding back on unleashing the risky leaps.

I was so proud of him.

Once your child has finished their last number, it is acceptable (I hope) to politely leave the theatre and make your way to the backstage door. I waited outside it for several minutes. The world within that door was not known to me, but after some minutes passed, I knew I was going to have to go get him. I took a deep breath and ventured in—to a world of hanging hose, hair ties and tiptoeing tiaras. In the chaos, I saw a glimpse of the Cricket King (his role in the performance) and made my move to intercept him. It was time to go.

The car ride from the theatre to our home is about twenty minutes after you get out of the city centre. The Cricket King sat in the back, which in retrospect was odd. Perhaps professional dancers have chauffeurs? I remember very clearly that he was in the back because my memories of what happened next are all of his face in the rear-view mirror.

There was an awkward, itchy silence. I could tell that there was a conversation dying to be born. It was that feeling you get when you know something needs to be said but nobody knows how to start. Finally, I reached out to the Feedback Model as some way of getting this going.

"What worked well for you today up there, Oz?"

With a simple, reliable question, I had unlocked the door. Out came the greatest list of his favourite features of his debut in the world of dance. Many of them I had seen. Several of them I had not, but now I knew them. He was so pleased to share them with me. And I was so relieved that I'd asked.

"What about tricky moments?"

A list just as long. And just as good. It wasn't negative; it just was what it was. Little mistakes. Big mishaps behind the stage. Dynamics that otherwise I would have never known about. And one tricky that I needed to pay special attention to.

"I was anxious to have you there, Dad. I know you wanted me to play hockey."

The weight of being a dad dropped on my head. I thought I'd been so careful and so clear about my belief in him and my support of him pursuing ballet. But I had obviously sent some signal, intentionally or not, that I was invested in something else. I was so happy that he'd said something.

"And what might you do differently next time?" I asked.

His level of sophistication in turning experience into learning was again striking as he provided a rigorous little list of the things he could work on next. But more than that was the expression of relief and delight on his face because I was interested in "next time." It was at that moment that I understood the spirit of feedback as a quality investment in someone raising their game, over and over again.

Now, I just had to live out my dream and provide some real-time feedback.

"Would you like some feedback from me?"

"Yes, Dad." (Close enough.)

I cobbled together a list of my favourite moments. And a list of the moments that looked a bit uncomfortable, along with a "do differently" that I don't remember. But I do remember I had the chance to say that he didn't need to worry about me wanting my kids to play hockey. I was over it. And I told him I was excited to watch him dance again.

An immersive, focused and honest conversation like that, convened soon after someone has thrown their heart into a moment of performance, is exactly the kind of conversation leaders are dying to have with (potential) mentors in their life.

TACTIC Delivering Performance Feedback

This tactic allows you to become a driving force in someone's desire to improve. Being the person in a social ecosystem who others can count on for honest and high-quality feedback brings people to your door with a range of exciting assignments. In essence, this tactic involves capturing high-quality feedback in your observations, having a system to keep track of the observations and being ready to share them in a rapidly created learning crucible.

TACTIC Shifting Positive/Negative Orientation

Some of the folks you work with will be drawn towards what's working well. They're glass-half-full people, and we love them for it. Others might be drawn towards what's not working well. Their glass is half empty, and we love them, too.

High-Quality Feedback
1 Highly Specific
2 Low in Judgment
3 Offered in Real Time

The Feedback Model
What worked **well**?
What was **tricky**?
What might you **do differently** next time?
Would you like feedback from me?
What I sensed worked **well**...
What I sensed was **tricky**...
What I might **do differently** next time...

It can be exciting to ask the kinds of questions that help balance out their default orientation. When someone is describing all the rainbows and unicorns in their life and how they're thriving, I might ask them a question like:

What's the most difficult part of being you these days?

When a mentee is describing a colleague they're incredibly frustrated with, I might ask:

What do you respect most about this person?

Questions from the orientation opposite to the one the person started with represent important moments in conversations. They represent that our desire is for the person in front of us to be honest, fair and comprehensive in their assessment. These are moments when a mentor can convey "I trust you" and "I sense there is more to this." They signal to our mentee that we're up for a real conversation—not a one-sided one.

REFLECTION

- What are three things you would like to be great at as a mentor?
- How and from whom could you arrange to receive feedback on each one?

MEDITATION
Move Straight Towards the Pain

Move straight towards the pain.
Even though every fibre of your being
is telling you it is someone else's place.
Move.
Be the first hand they feel on their shoulder—
the first hand between them and the cold, hard concrete.

Move straight towards the pain.
If that pain is hiding—
quietly inform it that you know it is there.
Assure it that it will not worsen in the light.
A wound unseen
remains untended.

Move straight towards the pain.
Thank it for the awareness it brings.
Carefully seek to understand it—even more.
Guard it from hurting more than it has to.

You cannot promise comfort.
But you can promise safety.

Move straight towards the pain.
Acknowledging what others
are pretending is not present.
Give the unspeakable its voice.
Let people say unpolished things.
Be the most honest person in the room.

Move straight towards the pain.
Go beneath it.
Put people in their finest light.
Be the person who puts every effort
into making their opponent
more articulate than they have ever been.

Move straight towards the pain.
Sit with others in their pain.
Find the truths and untruths in their stories.
Feel what they feel. Need what they need.
Uncover what they are making this mean about themselves.
So that they can move forward.

15

We Are Not Built for Easy

This is the true joy in life—being used for a purpose recognized by yourself as a mighty one. Being a force of nature, not a feverish, selfish little clod of ailments and grievances complaining that the world will not devote itself to making you happy.

GEORGE BERNARD SHAW

I'M WRITING this chapter during a month in South Africa with my daughter. For our last week here, we've graciously been offered the use of a client's family cottage in a place called Nature's Valley. The village is home to a pristine, kilometre-long beach, wrapped by the Indian Ocean and Tsitsikamma National Park (Tsitsikamma means "clear water" in the Khoisan language). Our home for the week is a *pondok*, or roundhouse, a largely open, fort-like brick circle with patios, plus windows and doors that open widely to let the summer in. You can hear the waves crashing on the pristine beach a stone's throw away. Hard to imagine a place more heavenly—or fun—for a family to spend time together in during the summer.

We're here, however, during the depths of a South African winter.

It would seem that only about 10 percent of the people who own cottages here use them at this time of year, which makes the streets quiet—and makes us wonder if this was such a good idea. The *pondok* has no heat. It's a very shaded, chilly place, particularly after 6 p.m., when the sun goes down. The humidity in the air makes it impossible to dry our clothes. Load shedding (scheduled state power outages) happens for a few hours every day at different times, and then we're in the cold and the dark.

The *pondok* also has no Wi-Fi, which has complicated my desire to get some writing done while we're here. We have jerry-rigged a system where one of our phones now has a South African sim card and a pay-as-you-go data plan that we can hotspot from—as long as we remember to keep the plan charged. We've had to top it up every few days by driving a treacherous little stretch of road to the top of the hill where a gas station sells us more data. I think they believe we might be mining for Bitcoin with the amount that we've purchased.

We pass the odd dog walker or trades van. Or the group of rangers who patrol the streets on bicycles to monitor and dissuade the local troop of baboons, an aggressive bunch, from breaking into cottages. In addition to coping with the cold and the dark, we're constantly scanning the forest around us for these expected intruders.

The truth is, my daughter and I have never had a better time together.

I'm reminded of a motto a friend once shared with me: "Not everything has to be fun to be fun."

We sip rooibos tea in the morning on the couch, wrapped in our sleeping bags. We do yoga on lime green mats we bought in town. We move the laundry rack around the yard to find patches of sunshine. We pack picnics. We play soccer on the beach and throw ourselves into rolling waves, knowing how good our one hot shower will feel before dinner. We sometimes stop for a milkshake at the Blue Rocks Café on our walk back from the beach. We cook and eat, drink wine and play cards from our sleeping bags by candlelight before packing it in—and doing it all over again the next day.

The discomfort of our experience in South Africa reminds me that we are not built for easy—an expression I once used in a magazine article about the COVID pandemic and the impact that it was having on people's mental health, especially as it stretched on. It's the sort of expression that my children make fun of me for creating. (They largely do this when they secretly like something I've said.) I wrote it to remind people that we are equipped with powers of buoyant grit and specialized mental states to take us through adverse conditions. Humans are designed to rise to the challenge in front of them with extra levels of focus, stamina and agility. We are built for purpose—and when that's our focus, we find our best. We also find happiness and success, mingled in with the inevitable sadness and failures that a life of purpose brings.

We are also not built to be alone. Which is the crux of this chapter.

When Things Don't Go as Expected

Mentorship requires that you have a strange attraction to situations where others are facing the pains of life—uncertainty, adverse conditions, disappointments. By calling it an attraction, I'm not saying you need to revel in these hardships as much as recognize them and automatically step towards them with compassion as you accompany people. The best mentors seem to invest their time and focus the way a savvy financial advisor invests their client's money: when times are tough.

When you see that someone is frustrated, agitated or overwhelmed, engage with them where they're at and describe what you are noticing. When you hear that someone is struggling, be in touch as soon as possible. Offer to get into it with them. When you sense that someone's facing a rocky transition or a challenging chapter, pledge a certain time, every week, to call them and touch base. Let them know that they're a priority to you, and that you're open to providing whatever they need most. When you feel someone has just taken a blow and is in pain, wrap them in the biggest, tightest hug you can, with all your heart and without hesitation. When tragedy strikes, and you're tempted to rationalize that giving someone space is what they really need, veto your rationalization and make your way to their doorstep. Override your instinct to hesitate. Cross the threshold of their front door and accompany them through their darkest moments.

You can give them their space when their healing is complete.

The Difference Between Safety and Comfort

It never ceases to amaze me how the subtleties of what words mean can shape radically different awarenesses and behaviours. The difference between *safety* and *comfort* is a prime example. In short, safety is at the heart of mentorship. Comfort is optional at best. Sometimes, comfort can actually get in the way of someone being all that they can be.

Comfort feels good. It's the feeling of a well-designed chair that gives your body a break from holding itself up. Or a warm meal that reminds you of your childhood. Comfort is the feeling of impeccable hotel service, where your every need is anticipated and taken care of. It's the confident feeling of delivering the part of a speech you know will make people laugh, because it has gotten laughs a hundred times before.

I'm not against comfort, just like I'm not against encouragement. Comfort and encouragement are good things. It is just that too much of good things without a balance can have unanticipated consequences. Like excessive encouragement, too much comfort stifles growth. It kills our appetite for learning and addressing challenges with a ready agility. It placates us. It bores us. It tames us to accept the status quo.

Safety and comfort must not be confused.

So many of the challenges that mentors work on with leaders involve the presence of safety and the absence (or irrelevance) of comfort. Intentionally building self-awareness is not comfortable. Learning how to give honest feedback—and take it—is not comfortable. Deep learning isn't, either. The weight of ownership isn't comfortable to bear. Staying true to one's values does not create comfort, and neither does risk, conflict, navigating change or aspiring to high performance. Even collaboration and innovation aren't comfortable if you're really going for it. And yet every single one of these endeavours requires safety.

A sense of legitimate psychological safety makes the mentorship connection possible. When mentors conduct themselves in a way that demonstrates vulnerability and pay deep attention to it in others,

The best mentors seem to invest their time and focus the way a savvy financial advisor invests their client's money: when times are tough.

---

those around them experience a freedom to be honest, to take risks, to learn and grow, to engage and connect, to contribute and to challenge. A mentor's conduct sends the paradoxical message that the person in front of them is extraordinary—yet has room to become more and more extraordinary each day.

A question stemming from the earlier chapter on conduct is, "How might I conduct myself in a way that creates this sense of safety, both around me and within others?" If we can shape ourselves to be the sort of person people feel safe with, then we may just earn the right to be confidants in their most uncomfortable challenges. And what else would a mentor want to be?

Opportunity in Conflict

Most people don't like conflict. It represents something to be avoided for the sake of harmony. But harmony rarely results when we avoid conflict. What's more likely is that we quietly entrench our positions, and the functioning of our partnerships diminishes. Trust erodes when we pretend that conflict is not there.

When people know that some sort of tough conversation is inevitable, they might reach out to a mentor for some help. Their motivation probably comes from the relief they expect to feel from having someone on their side—someone to complain to and convince that they are in the right. It's just the way our social brains are built. Misery loves some company. And we all love being right.

Experience with conflict is something every one of us has acquired along the way. This comes through loud and clear when we're helping someone navigate difficult situations. Just underneath our immediate urge to share similar challenges from our own past, there's an opportunity for a mentor to be more objective about what needs to be addressed. Rather than crawling down into the hole with your mentee, a mentor can use their curiosity to help the person they're working with reflect on, prepare for and engage in conflict in a way that creates a better outcome.

To do this, mentors need to understand the nature of conflict. They need to understand as much as possible about the situation at hand. And they need to have a few tools in their kit to help their mentee move forward effectively.

There are three ideas mentors need to understand about conflict. Think of it as an Olympic podium of mindset shifts that make finding opportunity in conflict easier. Each shift has a spot to stand.

The first mindset shift is between blame and contribution. Blame is a version of the story that gives one party full responsibility for what's gone wrong. It's where most of us go first in our initial analysis of a situation that's gone sideways. Blame makes things simple, and makes it clear who we can point the finger at as the reason for why we are where we are.

Contribution is a slightly more mature way to look at conflict. Who are all the people and what are all the factors that led to this situation? In an instant, we see that the responsibility is shared. A new team member isn't putting the required effort in to perform in their new role... *and* their manager hasn't taken the initiative to provide this feedback. For months. *And* the job description is ambiguous, not having enough specific standards mapped out. *And, and, and.* Now we have a much more complete understanding of why we're in this place. Mentors help people shift from a blame mindset to a contribution mindset, one where they can take responsibility for their contribution to a conflict and help others do the same.

Conversations with a mentor become like a bookmark, bringing us back to the place we last left off in our unfolding as a human.

The second shift is between intention and impact. Much like blame, intention is what we focus on when we're describing our own relationship to a problem from the inside out. Recognizing our impacts often takes a wider view. A board member takes a verbal jab at a colleague—half meant as humour, but half to identify a concern (intention). It causes some hard feelings in the colleague (impact) and makes them question their own value on the board (another impact). If we become involved in the conversation, it may be helpful to ask the colleague on the sharp end of the critique what they think their board member's intention was. Awareness of intention *and* an identification of impact would make further conversation on the subject much more productive.

Mentors can play an important role in helping their mentees understand this from both directions. Helping our mentees understand the intentions of others and providing them with the chance to be honest about the impact the other parties' actions have had often takes the sting out of moments of friction. Similarly, helping our mentees see some of the unintended impacts *they* are having allows them to address situations before they flare into conflict.

The third shift is between positions and interests. Positions are all the strong statements people make in conflict, often stemming from feelings of frustration, anger and being slighted. The fed-up customer says she'd like to speak with the manager. The school bus driver stops the bus, turns around and barks at his passengers to sit down and shut up. The exhausted business partner doesn't know what else to say except "we're done."

Interests, on the other hand, are what people actually *need* to move forward. They're elusive, humming just below the surface of what people are saying. The trained ear of a mediator is able to detect these interests, regardless of what people are *saying* they want. They can hear that the customer in the restaurant actually needs her dietary concern taken seriously. That the bus driver needs to concentrate on traffic to keep his passengers safe. And that the exhausted business partner needs a fairer division of responsibilities.

Mentors must help their mentees dig below positions to identify and articulate their key interests and become curious about the interests of others. If our mentees can help their "opponents" address their needs, they stand a greater chance of getting what they themselves need.

TACTIC Preparing Someone for Conflict

One of the most common topics that mentees will come to their mentors with is a source of conflict in their lives—something they believe needs to be addressed. A conversation with mentors can help them reflect and decide on their strategy for moving forward.

Identify the story: What is the story? What happened? What are the facts and events? Who are the characters involved? What else has contributed to this situation? What has been *your* contribution to this situation?

Identify the feelings: What are the feelings that have come up through all of this? What has been the impact on you? What might have been the intentions of the other parties involved?

What are you making this mean about yourself? What are you making this mean about the other parties involved?

Identify the needs: What are your needs going forward? What are your key interests? What do you suspect other parties might need? What does "good" look like when this is resolved? What does "great" look like? What is the fairest way to sum this situation up? How would you like to address this?

REFLECTION

- What conversations are needed in your life that will require courage to undertake?
- How safe would those involved feel to have these conversations with you?

MEDITATION
Every Person Has a Gift

Every person has a gift.
A genius bestowed at birth,
inherent and hidden,
lying in wait
for the conditions
that invite its unveiling.

Every person has a gift.
As difficult as it may be
for any of us to explain
or imagine what life would be
without it.
Those around us see it, clearly.

Every person has a gift.
Shining through the acetate,
finding its way to the screen.
Exposed in those seemingly unrelated scenes
where one's actions
pierce the impenetrable.

Every person has a gift.
An ability that, when uncaged,
sends a surge of impact
through the bedrock.
Making the difference
the world was waiting for.

Every person has a gift.
Polished and honed,
cherished and revealed,
tested in ever-increasing realms.
Relentlessly shared
alongside the gifts of others.

Every person has a gift.
Once found and named,
your life becomes its home.
Your days brim with the vocation
of being more and more and more
of who you have always been.

16

The Meaning of Life (Has Been with You the Whole Time)

The purpose of life is to discover your gift.
The work of life is to develop it. The meaning
of life is to give your gift away.
DAVID S. VISCOTT

MY YEARS at university were the time in my life when I learned the least.

You read that right.

Needless to say, my university alumni association won't be using that as a quote in their next publication. My time at university was more an exercise in perseverance, finishing something I had started. In retrospect, it was valuable—even to have experienced what it feels like to be going down the wrong road. At the time, it was excruciating. Chemistry labs were the bane of my existence. I couldn't wait for each day to come to an end. It was bad.

I've always dreamt of commissioning a sculpture on a university campus somewhere that captures how utterly daunting and confusing it is for a young person to think about their future. It would be called *The Way*. Looking at the sculpture from one end would be like looking into a vortex of jagged edges and incomprehensible connections. It would be a mystery how this jalopy of confusion didn't collapse to the ground. It would make a person feel lost and insignificant.

But from the other end—looking backwards from the future—it would be beautiful and smooth, every aspect of it guided by a simple and predictable pattern. It would look like an Airstream trailer version of a rocket ship: completely streamlined for space travel. It would serve as a heads-up to any student looking at it to let go of the chronic worry about where their life is going to end up. If you are open to it, life has a very methodical way of revealing your gift and helping you find a fun and meaningful way of using it to create impact, meaning and your livelihood.

Feeling Lost

At the age of 18, my perspective on what I would be when I grew up was mostly informed by what my parents did for a living, alongside my love of TV shows. My three favourite TV shows were *ER*, *L.A. Law* and *The Fall Guy*. I couldn't see myself as an accountant or a farmer (my dad was both), and being a nurse (like my mom) seemed pretty thankless. Which meant, in my mind, I had a choice to make between three TV careers: doctor, lawyer or stuntman. (I secretly wanted to be an actor, which of course would allow me to play doctors, lawyers *and* stuntmen, but didn't have the courage to go for it.)

The strongest daydreams I had of my future self were as a doctor: being kind and calm in delivering tough news to a patient and their family. I liked the idea of being steady and solid for people in these disruptive moments. I envisioned finding a way to inform families of the facts while also eliciting from them some measure of courage to move forward, regardless of how tough the news was. It was a strange appetite for a young man to have—helping people navigate through frightening territory. I was pretty sure it constituted a calling. And I was right. My vocation would just come wrapped in a different package.

I filled journals with my daydreams of working in small-town Saskatchewan and joining Médecins Sans Frontières to travel to drought-ravaged countries around the world. I told everyone I knew how badly I wanted to be a doctor, and why: to be with people at their most human moments.

In retrospect, these original daydreams were major clues for where meaning in my life was going to come from. At the time, I'd convinced myself that the only way I was going to have a meaningful life was by becoming a doctor. I was setting myself up for a major fall. I was in the wrong academic program and had blinders on for a path that was not for me. Sadly, and also with a lingering bitterness, there wasn't a single adult in my life who had the time, inclination or method to sit down with me, sift through my life and help me understand what my gift actually was.

Being Found

Except one.

Nancy Gibson was a professor in medical anthropology at my university. Any undergrad student could take her class as an elective. For me, it was as close as I could get to the medical faculty without actually being in medical school. It was a fascinating course about how culture influenced medical practices in Germany, France, the UK and the United States. In Germany, diagnosis and treatment centres on the heart and circulation. In France, the focus is the liver and detoxification. In the UK, it was all about the bowels and digestion. And in the US it didn't matter what your problem was—expensive and invasive surgery was the answer. Thirty years later, and I still remember Nancy's class.

More than that, Nancy noticed me. She probably noticed many of her students over the years, which I've learned is a rare and special gift for any educator to possess. She was interested in who I was, why I had signed up for her class and where I was headed in life. She was interested to find out what my gift was. And it was her curiosity that provided me with a lifeline.

When I confessed to her that my only aspiration for the future was to be a doctor, she suggested we go for a coffee. I sense she had met students like me before. I told her about my daydreams for the future. She was keen to find out about times in my past when I'd been at my best. She asked me about where I grew up and what that had been like. She wanted to know what I'd been good at and what my highest marks at university had been in (the answer was an elective in theatre!). She wanted to know the scenes in my life where I had shown up *exquisitely*.

And then she listened to everything I shared with her.

She explained to me that I might get into medical school, graduate and after a few years find that it wasn't for me. That I might be more interested in the team dynamics of hospital administration or innovation units or hospices. She said it sounded as if my gift was connected more to concepts and communication than to process and procedure. She pointed out that my disdain for chemistry labs may be a valuable sign that my mind was not as geared for the scientific process as it was attuned to leading people and ideas.

She helped me understand that I might have equated being exceptional in life with becoming a doctor. And that becoming a doctor would just make me a doctor. Becoming exceptional in my life would be more determined by knowing what my gift was, articulating that gift explicitly and designing my life around using it.

And if I didn't get into medical school, I would still possess my gift. It wouldn't be the end of the world.

Which, of course, is what it felt like when the rejection letters from medical schools came in. I had to go another way.

Knowing People Have a Gift

Nancy Gibson's desire to ascertain the gifts of her students represents an innate curiosity that quiet champions must possess. Helping mentees find and use their gift is one of the key outcomes they are focused on. Mentors need to believe that the leaders they work with possess a rare and distinct gift. They need to believe that this gift is very real, can be articulated and has the potential to accomplish incredible things in the world. Mentors need to help leaders pay attention to their gift and take it seriously. In a world that tempts people to believe they must be competent at everything,

It's as if mentors experience others through the question, "I wonder what their gift might be?"

---

mentors help leaders understand they will be more effective if they focus on and play to their strength. And mentors can help those they work with design their life around their gift.

It's as if mentors experience others through the question, "I wonder what their gift might be?"

I've been encouraged over the last decade by the growing trend in the personal development and career guidance space of focusing on one's strengths. It's a wonderfully refreshing convergence around the idea that no one can be excellent at everything. You can't even be competent at everything. Double down on what makes you uniquely gifted and design your life from there. Partner with others to make the offering complete.

Your gift is a superpower that you uniquely possess. It may be in the form of a talent, a strategy or an internal process that happens without you even trying, but it's something you are able to do that steers things in a different direction. Like the way a family counsellor diffuses the intensity of a conversation with their voice. Or a seasoned podcast host catches what seems like an ugly statement and opens it up into a surprisingly valid conviction. Certain surroundings and conditions bring gifts to life, allowing them to make a remarkable difference.

Everyone has a gift. Some people know what it is and use it every day. Others have caught glimpses of it in their life, but haven't reflected on what it is specifically and how it could be applied. Some don't sense a special gift or believe they have one. Their actions align with this belief, and they spend their days doing whatever work comes their way. An explicit awareness of one's gift allows a person to leverage it and refine it, intentionally.

Before jumping into finding your own and helping others find theirs, let's look at five key attributes of any leader's gift. This will identify what we are looking for and make the process easier to pursue.

A Gift Is Difficult for a Leader to See in Themselves

Because people have had their gift their whole life, it's very hard to imagine what life would look and feel like without it. They simply can't imagine not having it. It's a bit like trying to explain water to a fish.

I have a friend named Stephen. One of the reasons we're friends is that we have both found it challenging in life to "find our thing." At the time I was desperate to get into medical school, Stephen was determined to become a dentist. When that didn't work, he pursued forestry. Then he bought a restaurant and ran it for years, then sold it. After that he started the process for becoming a firefighter, before working with a company building log homes. Then he became an electrician, and now he also renovates homes. Beautifully.

He is really, really good at it. Which means *gifted*.

I've never heard Stephen articulate his gift, so I'm not sure how he would word it. But I would say Stephen sees space and the potential of life within it like nobody else I've ever met. He sees multiple layers of function and methodically imagines, measures and tallies which materials, tools and actions he will need to bring his inspiration to life. And then he creates it.

A Gift Is Something That Other People Notice

Gifts show themselves. They are not fabricated in the mind or something that can be wished into being. They exist and are therefore experienced by others. Chances are, bystanders won't be able to describe in detail what the gift is—they just know they appreciated how adept a person was in a certain situation.

Nina is our chief of staff at Roy Group. She leads our team and determines what we focus on as a small company. I met Nina twenty years ago as the corporate secretary for a college that I served on the board of. Nina embodies calm. Her standards are impeccable. As trustees, we always felt respected and appreciated, always felt the importance of what we were doing.

Decades later, it's very clear that what we noticed was Nina's gift at work. Her gift is in the way she listens and notices the nuances of situations and then communicates what is important. She quietly sends a clear signal that we have no time for nonsense. And that she believes we will get there (wherever that might be). I've seen her use her gift to align a room of strong egos, to coordinate our team to rally around a team member fighting cancer and to coordinate efforts to bring a political refugee and his family across the border from Afghanistan into Pakistan, late at night and against all odds. Nina's gift makes her a highly diplomatic operator in complex situations. Once you notice her gift, you can't experience Nina any other way.

A Gift Reveals Itself in Seemingly Unrelated Situations
Gifts are a bit like a mystery case that needs to be cracked. When given the chance to reflect on scenes in one's life where a person felt they were at their most exquisite, sometimes scenes emerge that initially don't seem to share a pattern. But the pattern is in there—a fingerprint of sorts being applied from a slightly different angle.

Roy Group has a client named Krista, who spent most of her late teens and 20s competing internationally as a snowboarder. In the feedback she received from a group of thirty people, a long-term teammate of Krista shared a story about snowboarding. A group of boarders had stopped above a complicated set of obstacles they had never undertaken to discuss the best way to approach and execute. Krista swooshed by them all, discerning her approach on the fly, adjusting in real time through the course and sticking the landing of her final jump in a way that made it look effortless. In that moment, she inspired everyone around her to go for it.

In another feedback example, which took place decades later, Krista hosted a large charity event that had brought out the city's good and great. Guests had understandably arrived out of obligation and duty, but left a few hours later fully engaged and committed to making exciting projects happen. Krista won them over with the way she conducted herself in those hours—the way she had prepared, the stories she shared and the way she treated people. They felt part of something important and meaningful. The event raised more money than anyone had thought possible.

Once again, Krista had navigated the situation in a way that inspired everyone around her. Her keen perception of whatever is in front of her, her grace in execution and the impact this has of warmly engaging and inspiring those around her to overcome the challenge at hand—it's a combination that wins the day. It is what she is gifted to do. And it shows up in all kinds of situations.

A Gift Creates an Impact That People Can Count On

It's one thing to count on a person for something they're good at. It is another to *know* they'll make it happen, because everything you've ever encountered about a person makes them uniquely suited for certain kinds of situations.

We have an associate named Donneil. She grew up in Jamaica and began her career in the hospitality and tourism sector, landing a key front-of-house post in the Bahamas. In sharing one of the scenes from her life when she was working at her best, Donneil talked about being the point person for hotel guests during a hurricane. Guests were understandably scared, disoriented and irrational. Incoming information was patchy and ambiguous. The threat of mass damage and the potential for injury were real and imminent. As uncomfortable as it sounds, these are exactly the conditions that invite Donneil's gift to appear. She quietly and methodically began to check in with each group of guests, sharing resources like water and blankets along with any new information she had.

In her work today, Donneil continues to have a unique relationship with adversity. It focuses her. She finds poise in the pressure and it builds levels of trust and connection with the people around her. She scans people's faces intuitively to see if they're struggling. She discreetly tends to whatever will help these people reconnect. The way she conducts herself allows people to feel as safe as possible, even in the face of scary realities. As it did that day of the hurricane, her gift has been used countless times since in her deep organizational work on justice, equity, diversity and inclusion. When the going gets really tough, Donneil guides people through the storm.

A Gift Is Something a Leader Never Gets Tired of Refining

A gift probably shows itself quite naturally in children, who are uninhibited by ideas of what smart, talented or gifted look like. Every time we leveraged our gift as kids, we liked how it made us feel and the impact it had on the world around us. So we started to use it as

Gifts are a bit like a mystery case that needs to be cracked.

---

a strategy as often as we could. We reached out and there it was, for us and everyone around us.

When the world sees us use it, they might give us a 10/10. But inside the experience of using our gift, we give ourselves an 8/10; we have a sense of what a 9/10 would feel like and look forward to the next chance to leverage it a little more. And it gets deeper and deeper as a theme in our life without us even trying.

I've always loved stories. I love movies and myths. For as long as I can remember, people have said I am a good storyteller. I love telling the extended versions of jokes and anecdotes—complete with details and exaggerated reactions.

But my gift is not as much about stories as about crafting and delivering phrases. I found my gift in the face of loss. Someone had to deliver my grandma Mary's eulogy. And my family asked me.

From the moment I was asked, something took me over—a desire to find the precise phrases that would give anyone listening the chance to know my grandma the way I did. I used the days before her funeral to immerse myself in conversations with the people who loved her the most. I fell asleep crafting phrases about her and dreamt about them. I woke up in the morning whispering the phrases I knew would honour her and scribbled them down on pieces of paper. I knew what I wanted to say and how I wanted to say it. I crafted phrases that made myself laugh out loud, and others that filled my eyes with tears. It turns out I'm a phrase guy.

And I suspect I always will be.

I love reading poetry and I love writing it. I use phrases to sell important ideas and influence the way forward. I use phrases to lead groups and when I work with clients on difficult challenges. I notice impactful phrases and the way other people deliver them. Sometimes I craft my phrases weeks in advance, and sometimes the moment before I speak. I'm trying my best to make this book full of the kinds of phrases that stir courage in honourable people—and to be with them in their most human moments.

Which, interestingly, is the exact reason I wanted to be a doctor all those years ago.

TACTIC **Distilling the Leader's Gift**

This tactic involves a process that might span over several conversations and take weeks or even months. It includes addressing the upcoming questions, and may involve crafting some clear assignments and getting your mentee to do some homework between sessions.

Work with your mentee to find a creative way to map out the story of their life.

- What is the unfolding story of my life to date?
- What have been some key ups and downs along the way?
- Where are all the places my story has been set in?
- Who have the key characters been?
- What beliefs have I acquired about life along the way?
- What themes have gotten deeper and deeper in me without any trying?

Help them identify and focus on a collection of scenes when they were at their best.

- What are seven to ten specific scenes from this story when I was at my most exquisite?
- What was the context that surrounded me in each one of these scenes?
- What were the actions I was capable of in each one of these scenes?
- What changes occurred around me when I took action in each one of these scenes?

Invite them to request some feedback from others.

- Who are thirty people who know me and have seen glimpses of my gift?
- How could I ask each of them to share a glimpse they had of me at my best?

- What was the context they saw surrounding me?
- What did they see me capable of doing?
- What changes did they see occur around me when I took these actions?

Work with them to wordsmith their gift.

- How would I articulate what it is I do when leveraging my gift?
- How would I articulate what changes around me when I use my gift?

REFLECTION

- Who are ten people you would like to assist in finding their gift?

MEDITATION
Entangle Yourself in Community

Entangle yourself in community.
Wrap yourself in the original human endeavour.
Sharing your gifts and ready presence with the young:
They are your promise to the world.
Sharing your gifts and steady presence with the elders:
They have kept their promise in you.

Entangle yourself in community.
Laugh out loud when people tell stories about being "self-made."
Pay attention in the moment to who you are shaping and who the forces are shaping you.
Stay connected with an eye on what is unfolding.
There is much to protect. And much to defend.

Entangle yourself in community.
Bring bundles of patience and understanding.
People arrive when they can.
Don't mistake imperfect for flawed.

The gathering has its own pace.
It brings everyone along.

Entangle yourself in community.
Like grasses twisted in the wind.
Like bull kelp twisted in the tide.
Every wave across the road,
every handshake and hug,
reminding us that we belong to this place.

Entangle yourself in community.
Make the table longer. And longer again.
Prepare more food than is required.
Care more than is considered wise.
Invite the outsiders in.
Waste time together in the most wonderful way you can imagine.

Entangle yourself in community.
Savour the moments that tip the scales.
Hearten yourself in the collective strength that will not yield.
Celebrate through day and night.
Do not go inside yourself—or go it alone.
Get each other safely home.

17

Get It Together, Together

The clear bead at the centre changes everything.
There are no edges to my loving now.
RUMI

A FEW TIMES every year, our team travels to Alberta to run development immersions with networks of mentors—the ThresholdImpact Venture Mentoring Service in Edmonton and the Venture Mentoring Service of Alberta in Calgary. We argue over who gets to go because it's always the kind of experience that prompts us to do our best work. Our day together with these networks always starts with a dinner the night before, where people share an example of someone who has earned the word *mentor* for them. The room is always full to capacity with as many people as we can possibly fit, and exactly the kinds of people we love working with: leaders in the community on the cusp of being mentors themselves.

In these immersions we dive into all of the themes we have outlined in this book: the primacy of conduct, the importance of practice and knowing what it is time for. We introduce the HELI model and the Feedback Model. We introduce the idea of helping leaders find their gift. And ways to address the tough stuff when it arises. Sharing a philosophy of mentorship and effective tactics with discerning practitioners who are hungry to learn is one of the great joys of my life.

They like it, too. The room is always full of laughter, sharing and connection. These networks in Alberta have created something very purposeful and social—it honours a mentor's desire to learn, belong, contribute and achieve something excellent as a team.

The Venture Mentoring Service concept was created by MIT and launched in 2000, the same year I found myself in way over my head on the Isle of Skye. Little did I know that the dynamic I was experiencing on Skye—a young entrepreneurial leader surrounded by a constellation of deeply invested mentors—is exactly what MIT had carefully designed as its recommended mode for developing the kinds of leaders who create wealth, livelihoods and community. They saw mentorship as essential, transformative when at scale and a game-changer in the lives of high-potential entrepreneurs.

The Alberta chapters are two of over 130 chapters across North America and now around the world. They have identified a few key design principles to stay true to:

Mentorship is a team sport. Each entrepreneur enrolled in the program is provided with a small and dedicated team of three or four carefully selected and highly developed mentors. These mentors meet regularly (normally monthly) to serve as confidential counsel, bringing together different backgrounds, experience, know-how and perspective. Together, they focus on the issues, challenges, aspirations and growing capacity of their entrepreneur as they develop their own venture in turn.

It's about the jockey, not the horse. The venture is recognized as the vehicle for entrepreneurial learning and development—but the entrepreneur themselves is the primary focus. If a given venture doesn't succeed, research suggests that the entrepreneur in question will start another one (and continue to become someone that their community can count on). This focus is so clear that mentors are not allowed to financially invest in the venture, to avoid any conflict of interest.

Mentorship is free. There are no fees or memberships in this model. There are also relatively few costs because all of the mentors are volunteers. People commit their time and their energy to the process. Someone always picks up the tab for coffee. Everyone involved is there for the right reasons.

These three simple design principles have helped create the single most engaging, effective and sustainable mentorship initiative I have ever experienced. They have also transformed a deeply embedded mental model that limits the impact of mentorship.

Not Going It Alone

For many of us, a mentor relationship is something that's one-on-one. Mentor and Telemachus. Founder and protégé. Master and apprentice. Seasoned veteran and bright-eyed rookie. Today it's mentor and mentee.

If the reason you picked up this book is because you are beginning this journey, let me lay down one important piece of advice: Don't go it alone.

Someone once explained to me how GPS works. When my phone is connected to a single satellite, it can estimate my location from the angle and distance with an accuracy of within a few hundred feet. If my phone can connect to two satellites, the signals triangulate and my location can be identified more accurately—say, within one hundred feet. If a third satellite gets involved, we create a pyramid of three dimensions. It's in this array of reference points that one can really know where they stand, within inches. This is the same principle that allows a hiker to use multiple mountain peaks and a compass to accurately place their location on a map. And this principle points to how we need to provide navigational guidance to our next generation of leaders.

Find a community of mentors. Connect with other mentors. Connect with *your* mentors and let them know you have found the path. Connect with people who have been mentors a long time, and with people who are just getting started on this journey with you.

Welcome people in from the wilderness. Get people together to talk about mentorship. Talk about the void. Talk about the *zugunruhe*. Share articles that you find interesting. Make requests to each other and promises. Be a resource to each other. Share your triumphs *and* your train wrecks. Turn meetings into meals together. Zealously refer each other to interesting people for a chat. Laugh together and learn together. Become friends. Help each other become memorable characters in the stories of other people's lives.

Together.

Don't limit the contact with your mentees to a clinical hour online once a month, either. Introduce them to each other and to your family. Go on outings with other mentors and their mentees. Go to the movies and talk about what it all means. Find a boat and take it out for the day. Criss-cross paths with each other. Introduce them to other mentors you trust. Invite everyone involved to a barbecue to meet each other. Introduce your mentees like they are guests of honour, describing the specific attributes that you find remarkable in them. Make toasts to them. Let them make toasts to you. Thank people for spending time together.

Community is what you have been looking for. To be surrounded by a community is what emerging leaders will need most. Community, and our ability to create it everywhere we go, is what is going to make re-finding our future possible. Use the way you conduct yourself to create community. That is what mentors do. Mentorship (and leadership, for that matter) are human dynamics that come from the realm of community. Long before there were guilds, factories and enterprises—even before there were governments—there was community. And it is in being wrapped in this spirit of community that our next generation of leaders needs us most.

Business did not create these concepts. Business *borrows* these concepts to accomplish its goals. And it is wise to do so. For decades I have watched something special happen to the cultures within organizations that cultivate mentorship. When leaders, managers and supervisors do what they need to do to earn the word *mentor*, problems like compromised performance and low engagement start to

If you picked up this book because you are beginning this journey, let me lay down one important piece of advice: Don't go it alone.

---

disappear. When leaders choose to become mentors consciously and begin playing for each other, everyone involved finds deeper levels of connection, purpose and meaning in their efforts. People feel safe to take risks. They accomplish more than they ever thought possible. Succession takes care of itself, and organizations become story engines for tales of collaboration and innovation.

TACTIC **Convening Wise Council**

Wise Councils are a favourite Roy Group ritual and epitomize the way mentorship can function beyond the limits of a one-on-one relationship. The ritual consists of the person who is the focus of the council (perhaps your mentee) and three to six council members who are selected based on their availability and connection to the topic, mentee or both. A strong council consists of a diverse group of people with different lines of sight on the issue.

Wise Council consists of four phases.

Phase 1: Setting the Table

The mentee outlines their area of focus—a dilemma, a decision, an aspiration. They are not interrupted as they update the council on all relevant details and dynamics connected to their focus, and what they believe the crux of their issue is.

Phase 2: Disciplined Inquiry

Council members ask both clarifying questions (to confirm and uncover key facts) and probing questions (which are more conceptual and nudge the mentee to dig a little deeper into their topic). Council members can build on each other's questions and gently interrogate anything that was tabled.

Phase 3: Behind Your Back

The mentee turns their chair around so that their back is to the council. They have an open notebook on their laps and are able to make notes of any relevant comments that occur "behind their back" as the council has a frank discussion, pretending that the mentee is not present and hearing it. Council members can talk openly about what they heard and saw during Phases 1 and 2, wonder about what might really be going on and what this is connected to or ideate about ways forward. Normally, this section is rich with new insights for the mentee.

Phase 4: Resetting the Table

The mentee turns back around and explains how they see their issue now: which insights they think are valuable, and reasons why other insights aren't as relevant to them. If the right action is now clear to the mentee, they can share how they intend to move forward. If it isn't, they can outline any next steps they intend to take based on what has been unearthed by the Wise Council experience.

A specific amount of time is allocated to the ritual, based on the seriousness and nature of the topic. This total time allotment is then allocated between the four phases.

For example, a simpler topic might get twenty minutes in total, split up like this:

- Setting the Table: 3 minutes
- Disciplined Inquiry: 7 minutes
- Behind Your Back: 7 minutes
- Resetting the Table: 3 minutes

A more serious or complex council session might get two hours, allocated as follows:

- Setting the Table: 20 minutes
- Disciplined Inquiry: 30 minutes
- Break: 10 minutes
- Behind Your Back: 30 minutes
- Resetting the Table: 30 minutes

Wise Council

1
Setting the Table
Outlining an area of focus.

2
Disciplined Inquiry
Questions to clarify. Questions to probe.

3
Behind Your Back
Noticings. Wonderings. Insights. Ideas.

4
Resetting the Table
New clarity. Different perspectives.
Action.

Moving at the Pace of Community

The modern world has a tendency to glorify efficiency—but efficiency tends to limit our ability to connect with what is most important.

If engineers were asked to change the path of a stream flowing through a relatively flat landscape, they would use an impressive array of factors to calculate the depth and width of an arrow-straight trench between point A and point B. I don't doubt that they would be able to move the water from A to B as efficiently as humanly possible.

But there would be no life in their trench. It would just drain the water away. We love straight lines from A to B. We love predictability, logic and streamlined processes. We like putting the least amount in to squeeze the most value out. We love it when someone tells us to work smarter, not harder. We minimize time sinks, energy drains and wastes of money. Landing things on budget and on deadline will make you a rock star project manager. It may even land you a seat at the top table.

Having a clear system for how you use your time—and I mean, *all* of your time—is another all-important signal to the world that you have your act together. Welcome to the efficiency trench.

When nature moves water through a landscape, it has a wonderful habit of taking full advantage of whatever is. Water carves a path that snakes its way between A and B via geological opportunities like subtle grade changes and weaknesses in the substrate. It follows its nose.

The great benefit nature has without efficiency as a primary design principle is the magic of life. The twists and turns create pockets of sunshine and shadow. Rate and depth and circumference of turn are all unstandardized, creating stages and eddies of solace for nutrients to settle, grasses to grow and eggs to attach to objects. The depths of its silt and sands are an unpredictable canvas of festering ooze and foul-smelling slimes. Rays of sunshine expose twisted, slippery, algae-caked roots that spend most of their day in the shadows. Until the night, when all kinds of sleeping creatures wake up to feed and leave their mucus on any surface that will take it.

It is not pretty or perfect. But it is in this belly of life that time, energy and materials cycle around and around. Nucleic acids replicate and the experiment continues, as it has done for millions and millions of years, (very) effectively creating the conditions for its own existence and for transfer to the next generation.

Life doesn't design things in straight, "efficient" lines as much as it builds things in highly effective articulated curves. It doesn't worry about the cleanliness of lines, preferring an unfathomable messiness. It maximizes surface area whenever it can for contact between life forms. After 3.7 billion years on Earth, it would be hard to argue that nature is not the world's greatest innovation lab for what actually works.

As mentors, we need to work the same way.

Mentorship Is Effective, Not Efficient

Mentorship is not efficient.

If you can let go of the desire for it to be efficient, you'll leave space for the good stuff. It will breathe life into your relationships with mentees and other mentors alike.

Mentorship is the oxbow creek snaking back and forth, bringing us back frustratingly near to the place we have just come from. Sometimes barely moving, and sometimes full and overflowing its banks. It is muddy, messy and filled with alluvia that will consume a rubber boot when given the chance.

Mentorship takes time, in the same way that nature does, to build things that last. It requires nurturing the sources of relationship, and creativity and trust. It happens on road trips, on long walks and over shared meals. It happens when we have time to burn with someone for no predetermined reason. The spirit of mentorship shows up when we have time to share what we are noticing and learning about. It enters the room when we set the agenda aside, perhaps just for a moment, and are surprised by where the conversation goes. It knocks on Saturday morning when we had other things planned. It happens in late-evening reviews of the long, tough, iterative initiatives that our critics said would never work.

And there are things we can do as mentors that invite this essence of mentorship into moments. Through practice, we can learn how to bring Athena's signature presence—being highly aware of ourselves, our conduct and the story that created us, combined with a disciplined ability to move the bead of our focus to the emerging experience of someone else. We know how to flip the switch inside to fully recognizing the person we're with as someone who is important to us, and talk about something that is important to them. We know how to send signals to someone that we enjoy being with them, even though what we are talking about is uncomfortable and challenging. We know how to breathe to stay grounded, solid and steady for someone. Even when we don't have extra time, we know how to act like we have all the time in the world, even for just a moment or two. It's in these moments that Kairos stops the clocks and asks us what it's really time for.

Mentorship takes up all kinds of valuable time. It requires checking in with people about how they are before diving in to solving problems. It requires asking questions that don't have simple answers. It requires asking people about their families, and trusting our intuition to take the conversation into sensitive, vulnerable and unpredictable places. It requires time that the world will tempt you to believe is being wasted—because it is time that you could use to do big and impressive things in your own life rather than invest in someone else's.

Mentorship requires initiative, thoughtfulness and commitment—creating connection across a million in-between moments that mean nothing now and everything later. It means patiently sitting with people when they go back to where we've already been, combing through evidence that we have clearly established is not "true." Any clear objectives get blurred and combined with everything that it means to be human. A deteriorating marriage hinders someone's ability to focus. Deep-seated insecurities find their way into a conversation and take it sideways. Executing to plan is complicated by an inexplicable sadness that will not go away.

But it is also the days together, not just the hours, when we can hear what is real for someone else. When a knotted mess of yarn they have been dragging along gets untangled. They find the right way forward for them because of time with us. And we laugh, or cry, or argue, or be silent together about everything else going on in our lives. So we leave knowing who the other person is, and they know us. And that they are with us.

So put away your office shoes and put some boots on. Phone someone up and ask them if they'd like to burn a day together. Or two. Choose to cook a meal together that isn't easy to pull off. Have an espresso after dinner and stay up late talking. Embrace inefficiency. Embrace what emerges. And experience the most effective strategy for human development the world has ever known.

Have Fun, Together

When I think about that constellation of mentors who came out of the woodwork for me in my mid-20s in Scotland, it is very clear

Mentorship is not efficient. If you can let go of the desire for it to be efficient, you'll leave space for the good stuff.

---

what made them so effective in impacting the trajectory of my life. They were not just a collection of individuals. They were in it together. They functioned as a guild. They challenged each other and supported each other (and me). They learned together. They liked discerning and doing the right thing together. They looked out for each other (and for me). They enjoyed spending time together (and with me). They laughed together. They relished challenges together. They liked focusing together and making big stories happen in the world. And they had fun investing their time and energy in me, together.

I see groups of mentors doing this for people in every corner of a community. I see two young entrepreneurs having early-morning breakfast with the business veteran they trust. I see a senior fundraiser surrounded by her team, going through lists and taking the time to share stories about what has worked and what hasn't. I see two titans of industry who I can tell have been at that table before—perhaps it's the place they like to meet up—but today they brought a young man to join them, and they are asking him what he is noticing in the world.

When leaders are surrounded by mentors like this, those who look to them for leadership will not be let down. Our ability to entangle ourselves in these connections, to gain this credibility and wield this influence, is one focused on liberating remarkable people from fear so that they can reign over the moments of their life.

It is an act that entails zero authority. Each of us really only has sovereignty over the moments of our own life. So this hunger you may be feeling is about connecting very deeply with people. Connecting in a way that makes you a credible source of counsel, which will allow you to influence how consciously others make their choices. Unless we weave people together in this way, they will keep making decisions that are private, secret and exposed to all of the forces that appear when we are isolated.

Your credibility might come from the incredible things you have accomplished, the depth of your learning, your reputation for being a top-shelf person who people can trust. It's probably a combination of these things. And that gets you a spot at the table. From now on, you might need to be a bit more conscious, discerning and deliberate about how you play your cards to maximize the influence you can have. As you've seen since we embarked on this journey together, I've written this book to help you be conscious, discerning and deliberate.

It is our connection to others, specifically as a resource for the next generation, that fuels our evolution. It is this collection of connections that holds us to account and brings a higher level of decision-making and governance to the choices that count in our lives and impact the lives of others. It's this small but carefully curated collection of characters who ground us in our finest self so that we can make our finest contribution, again and again. Mentorship supports humanity's finest desires and challenges our most limited thinking. It jars us from our neurological ruts to find new perspectives. Mentorship is a dynamic that invites us to be responsible for things bigger than ourselves. We may not always like it, but we respect and trust it. And we need it.

REFLECTION

- Who are three other mentors you would like to share this journey with?
- What would be your favourite place to meet with them?
- How often would you like to get together to do that?

MEDITATION
Be Discerning

Be discerning.
Alive to what is around you,
and within you,
and what that requires
in the here, now and this
for you to be.

Be discerning.
Keen to gently acknowledge
each nuance,
each signal through the noise.
Open to each and every sense,
pattern and layer of what is.

Be discerning.
Ready with a clear "no"
to any ragged and uninspired designs
that do not meet the moment.
Staying true to those protocols
you have crafted for your own finest self.

Be discerning.
Mindful of your beliefs
knowing that they might change.
Heartful in your convictions
knowing that they may evolve,
over time.

Be discerning.
Resolute in the words you select,
and how you choose to use them.
Grounded in the phrases
that you create
to stir courage and make way.

Be discerning.
Take everything you have ever noticed
and place it carefully in this moment,
without a thud or a crash.
Like a candle on the windowsill
to guide others through the storm.

Conclusion:
Why I Wrote This Book

*We teach what we need to learn.
And we teach it until we get it.*
IRENE TOMKINSON

SEVERAL YEARS BACK, following the publication of his critically acclaimed book *In the Realm of Hungry Ghosts*, Dr. Gabor Maté addressed a packed auditorium. He spoke of his writing process.

"I start," he said, "knowing that I never want to write a book that the world doesn't need."

His conviction stuck with me for years. To my core, I had zero desire to add to the noise.

But I believed thousands of people might need this book. Starting with me.

When I look forward into an increasingly volatile world, it's hard not to be overwhelmed. We face some wickedly complex dynamics. It's clear that as a species, we're going to have to raise our game. We are going to need quantum leaps in our development—as individuals, as teams, as communities and as societies.

Levels of predictability are crashing. It feels to me like there are death stars being built in every corner of the sky. And those are just the ones we know about. The questions become: "What force at our command is strong enough to give us a fighting chance? Is there some dynamic that might begin to roll the way we need it to, and with steadily increasing momentum? What glimpse of the familiar have we overlooked? What whispers of the obvious have we not paid attention to, until now?" And further, "how can this X factor be distilled, amplified and enhanced?"

Our next generation of leaders will need more than being paired up with willing volunteers with some time on their hands. Making sense of, navigating through and learning from their experience as it emerges requires a committed council of mentors that they trust and learn to tend to. Together, everyone involved needs to follow the elegantly crafted *how* to this process regardless of any *what* that comes their way.

More than anything else, mentors will need to create space for the conversations that are dying to be born: conversations about fear, failure and frustration. They cannot be the kinds of people who take up all of this space themselves.

We all need to surround ourselves with the kinds of people who dare us to engage wholeheartedly and find the most meaningful way forward. We need others to help us recognize patterns, contemplate layers of ethics and consequence, and run the kinds of experiments that just might reveal that path. Every entrepreneur, scientist, public servant, mother, uncle, artist and CEO will need to be surrounded with a carefully curated council of mentors. Then they, and we, can go and create the triumphs we never dreamt were possible.

Becoming these quiet champions for the next generation, together, represents the greatest influence our lives will have on steering humanity towards a better place.

MEDITATION
Be Agile in Your Conversations

Be agile in your conversations.
Pay close attention.
Every conversation is an uncracked case,
fraught with tiny clues about what is possible.
See where your next statement will take things
and do not miss your chance to land it.

Be agile in your conversations.
Be methodical.
Confirm what is obvious.
Relay it back.
Identify what we do not know.
Prepare to get lost and confused together.

Be agile in your conversations.
Honour someone's poetry when it is spoken.
Hear the repetition of what they need to say.
Crawl into the caves of their metaphors.

Interrogate symbols until they whisper what they represent.
Shiver or sweat in the temperature of every phrase.

Be agile in your conversations.
Make ground as hastily as possible.
And as slowly as is required.
Do not look at your shoes when emotions arrive.
Sit with them—sit with all of them.
And listen to what they say to each other.

Be agile in your conversations.
Let your precision only seem casual.
Thrust your spear to spin the planet another way.
Do not miss with the things you say.
Point to what is clearly in the light.
Wonder about what is in the shadows.

Be agile in your conversations.
Listen for fleeting requests and promises.
Sense the patterns beneath the surface.
And when the moment arrives
that needs your voice…
please say something worth remembering.

Acknowledgements

IN MANY WAYS, this entire book is an acknowledgement—of a special human dynamic that has made me a better person over the course of my life. Every conviction within this book comes from patterns I have noticed in a group of exquisite people who have accompanied me over the past five decades, or from the stories others have shared about the people who have accompanied them. When we were young, their attention invited us out into the world. As we got older, they gave us glimpses of example that we have emulated and added to the way we try to be in the world. They are not perfect people, but if we have used the word *mentor* to describe them, it speaks to their generosity, honesty and investment. They have passed the torch and helped us find our path. Like we can now do together for others.

I'm guessing my mom and dad, Heather and Michael Chisholm, would say their moms (Wendy and Mary) and dads (Jim and Roy) were their first mentors in the same way I'd say my mom and dad were mine. There's no question that my grandma Mary and grandpa Roy's sisters, Angeline and Eveline, were mother figures to my mom (who tragically lost her own mother when she was 17). My mom will also tell you that my grandpa Roy was a mentor to her, perhaps stepping into the space that her own dad had a hard time occupying in the second half of his life.

I landed a legendary collection of aunties and uncles—Helen and Garry Fletcher, Robin Hoffman and Ian Chisholm, Judy and Tom Drury, Mary and Doug Reynolds—who let me know that they were invested in who I was becoming. As did a wider group of people who we called aunties and uncles like Madeline and Alfred Comeau, Lynn and Chuck Moser, and Sharon and John Milligan (though one sad day we found out these were honorary titles, not biological ones).

As we grow and develop, we start to collect a crew of adults who we can count on, and if we're lucky, they help us figure out who we are—both as individuals and as members of our families. I was so fortunate to have this wider circle of adults who somehow signalled to me that they were in my corner. These were people like Ray Nelson, who I mentioned in the introduction; special teachers in high school like Candace Koziski and Orest Gluckie; and the incredible leaders that Operation Enterprise introduced me to like Brian Hesje (who I miss every day), Pete Cohen, Dave Sullivan, Suzanne and Tom Cronkite, and Sue and Ron Myers (who I mentioned in chapter 9). Venturing even farther from home during an exchange year, working for Jack Bruce at Laing's Bar in Dundee, Scotland, taught me more about business than any degree ever could have.

When I look back through the story of my life, I can see that the quantum leaps in my development as a leader (and a human) happened in the presence of mentors. For whatever reason, they each at different times intercepted my trajectory, staying close for a chapter or two of my life. Some have shown me the kind of leader I would like to be in the world, like Tony Fields (who you met in chapter 5) and Rod Stewart Liddon (from chapter 7). Some continue to provide me with glimpses of the kind of person I want to become, like Tim Gallwey (from chapter 5), Peter Hill (chapter 10) and John McAreavey (chapter 12). Others have shown me ways I *don't* want to be. I've lost track of a few over the years. There are some I speak to every month like Robert Henderson and Mark Bell (to whom this book is dedicated). There are two I have learned alongside from the moments they arrived—my brothers Bradley and Stephan—who inspire me as quiet champions in our families, businesses and communities.

I am specifically conscious of how many of the stories I've chosen to share in this book come from a single decade of my life. This theme was echoed in many of the stories I've heard others telling about their mentors: that they seem to show up at exactly the time we need them to. For me it began at university, where I struggled. I am so grateful to have lived at St. Joseph's College and to have had upperclassmen like Phil Heaton (who I miss every day) and Dusty Read and resident mentors like Father Jeff Thompson, Father Steve Lacroix, Father Bob Barringer, Father Russ Pedergast, Father Francis Firth and Father Tim Scott. When I failed to get into medical school I was devastated. As this had been my single goal at university, I needed to recalibrate—something that had already started thanks to Dr. Nancy Gibson (from chapter 16). I ended up taking some unexpected assignments that carried me far from my family and my home, to the eastern seaboard of America and back to Scotland. But I was not alone.

From the moment we first met at Mitchell Point, I have been continuously learning from the way Anne-Marie Daniel conducts herself as a professional, a partner, a parent and an innovator. Accompanying her in this lifetime has made me a much better leader. My admiration for Anne-Marie's philosophy, practice and skill set as a mediator has deepened over decades of watching her in action. She is unfazed in the face of heated arguments, assisting opposing parties to articulate their positions and graciously helping people get through tough deliberations. I've also been very fortunate to meet her mentors in the field—people like Alice Estey, Lee Bryan, Yvonne Byrd, Harvey Golubock, Jim Suskin, Lee Suskin, Susan Terry, Linda Stein, Larry Mandel and Neal Rodar—the people she learned her craft from. The realm of conflict mediation is a growing field where seasoned practitioners spend their life learning from and with each other.

Anne-Marie's parents, Sir John and Kristin Daniel (who I miss every day), her uncles Peter Daniel and Tom Scheidler, and aunties Ginny Truelove, Alison Daniel, Andrea Scheidler, Rondi Lightmark and Erica Swanson are most certainly in the constellation of mentors I keep around me.

A few of the mentors who accompanied me in those formative years of leadership came with me from my time with Operation Enterprise and the American Management Association International in the US. Peter Hill, Graham Houston and Kirsty Leishman at The Industrial Society all stepped up for me, as did Tony Morgan and Neil Wragg at Youth At Risk UK. They were excited for me and invested in me. When Columba 1400, the leadership centre on the Isle of Skye, hired me as its first CEO, it also unknowingly acquired my network of mentors. They were implicitly part of the deal.

Some of these mentors were people I reported to in the organization's board of directors. The Columba 1400 board had been meticulously curated and was ably chaired by our founder, Norman Drummond, who understood governance, leadership and all that it would take to position a young CEO to succeed in a challenging mission. The board put me in touch with an incredible collection of quiet champions like our patron HRH the Princess Royal, Barry Ayre (a very special mentor to me), Olive Ayre, Elizabeth Drummond, Julia and James Ogilvy, Geraldine and Stuart Mitchell, John Moorehouse, Liz McAreavey, Angus Ross, Bill Barr, Gourlay Fairman, Elizabeth Coffey and Graeme Crawford. Sitting around a table four times a year behind closed doors to report on progress and convince each other of the best way forward is one of the greatest learning experiences I've ever encountered. Playing for each other outside those closed doors, the way our wider Columban team did, created a remarkable chapter in an organization that continues to flourish more than a quarter-century later.

Some of these mentors had no logical reason whatsoever to step up for me the way they did. Stevie Seigerson came across from the Greater Easterhouse Development Company, where our early work with Stuart Miller and the GEDC team had been pivotal. I had quiet champions as neighbours—Alastair "Crookie" (who I miss every day) and Amy Cruikshank, Jackie Clark (who I miss every day) and Violet Fenton, Dolly McKinnis, Meg and Lachie Gillies, Jane Ross, Sine Gillespie and Donald MacDonald. There were leaders in that community I learned from like Robert Muir, Campbell Grant, Anne Martin and John Whyte. And leaders in Scotland like Donald Dewar,

Wendy Alexander, Sir Tom Hunter, Robert Crawford, Susan Rice, Lesley Riddoch and Ruth Wishart.

Looking back, I'm amazed by the realization that many of these mentors were around the age I am now—just into my 50s. I'm only now fully understanding how valuable their contribution was and the sacrifice they made to play the role they did. My children were young; theirs were entering adulthood. My organization was a start-up riddled with challenges; theirs were more sophisticated and at critical junctures of evolution. My marriage was brand new; they were a few decades in and experiencing the things that relationships do with time. There was a lot at stake from week to week—and yet they still chose to show up as potent characters in the story of my life. They invited me into their homes and lives. They gifted their time to me. They gifted their focus. Some were hard on me, holding me to high standards, but it was always about putting their attention and effort into the Ian Chisholm project. They *accompanied* me.

It was hard to leave this mentor-rich environment and return to Canada. An invitation from Diana Maughan to join the board of directors of Pearson UWC gave me the opportunity to find a new constellation of leaders to learn from: Francis Saville, Randy Gossen, Susan Green, Sue Voigt, Emma Howard Boyd, Julie Payette, Jim Hayhurst, Kahlil Shariff, Michael Pearson, Chuck Burkett, Lisa Ryan, Joe Clark and David Hawley. As Roy Group began to find its feet, quiet champions came out of the woodwork. Lynda Haverstock, Barbara Brown Herman, Karyn Purvis, Alison Meredith, Marilyn Taylor, Nowell and Jeanne Donovan, Mike Slattery and David Cross were excited to have me back on this side of the pond. Allen and Gwen Edzerza had time for me. Shelly Berlin and Richard Eaton had time for me. Shelly Sullivan, Doug Konkin and Judi Beck had time for me. Bob and Linda Chartier had time for me. Andre Mamprin, Ross Gilchrist and Janet Alford had time for me. Bob Snowden, Brent Hesje, Billy Moores and Dave Mowatt had time for me. Kim Campbell, Martin Ferguson-Pell and Ray Muzika had time for me. Ted Kouri and Jared Smith had time for me. It's humbling to consider just how much these folks have done for me. Or who I would be if they hadn't. There would be no Roy Group without these characters.

There would also be no book without a special group of quiet champions. I must first thank the Roy Group team and our chief of staff, Nina Moroso, who have stepped up and taken on so much to create the space for me to take on this project. My hope is that this book will help us have all kinds of fun and fulfillment in the years ahead.

I need to thank David Snowden and The Cynefin Co. for allowing my team and me to use the power of Sensemaker as a research tool. With the help of Julie Cunningham and Vivienne Read from Complexability Australia, and Dr. Sarah Fletcher, I believe we found some important truths locked up in the stories about mentors that people carry around. I'd like to thank Dan Coyle, Michael Levine, David C. Baker, Dan Pontefract and Jill Payne for agreeing to speak with me early on in the process and for being so frank about the experience of writing a book.

I am so grateful to the incredible leaders who championed my writing sabbatical in 2023: Zita Cobb and her Shorefast team for my time on Fogo Island; Chief K'odi Nelson and his team at the Nawalakw Healing Society for my time in Alert Bay; Rob Taylor and Tracy Hackland and the team at Columba Leadership in South Africa; and Marie Clare Tully, Jackie Gillies and the team at Columba 1400 on Skye. My conversations with you have shaped my convictions about just how valuable mentorship is.

Alex Van Tol is simply the most talented book coach I could have ever worked with on this book. Her curiosity, discernment, method and patience have helped me become more as a person. Emily Schultz and David Marsh took this rookie writer through his first editing process in the most creative, dignified and professional experience I could imagine. And Jesse Finkelstein believed so passionately that the world needed this book that she put the incredible Page Two publishing team behind that belief.

I am so thankful for the many Athenas who have dropped down into my life.

MEDITATION
Stop Yourself from Interrupting Magic

Stop yourself from interrupting magic.
Shine the silver. Set the table.
Communicate without a word
that what will happen here is important.
When the guests arrive—show them to their place
and disappear.

Stop yourself from interrupting magic.
Clock its movement towards the moment that counts,
but say nothing as it passes you.
The magic is focusing itself to do what it must do.
Bring the food and water without a sound
so as not to interrupt the weaver and her piece.

Stop yourself from interrupting magic.
If you have been wise,
you have already done what you needed to do.
Sorting through all the doubts and fears,
sifting the wheat from the chaff.
Readying and steadying others to unleash.

Stop yourself from interrupting magic.
The finest thing you could possibly do now
is note every single shred of what unfolds.
Every movement and every tone.
Every break of luck and wobble of fate.
Take. It. All. In.

Stop yourself from interrupting magic.
Your time will be after the magic has departed.
Pull them to the side—pull them together
and convene the after-action review.
Help them understand what they experienced.
And then share your notes.

Stop yourself from interrupting magic.
You are an inviter, a steward and a protector of potential,
convening the conversations that people need to have
before and after they play their hearts out.
Getting better and better and better.
The greatness comes from them.

About the Author

IAN CHISHOLM is a founder and partner of Roy Group, a "small giant" leadership development firm founded in 2004. Roy Group uses research, experiential learning and integrative team practice to work with organizations in developing their next generation of leaders by developing their senior leaders as our next generation of mentors.

Originally from Saskatchewan, Chisholm began his career with the American Management Association International's Operation Enterprise division, working closely with the US Postal Service and inner-city high schools to bring young talent from tough socioeconomic realities into immersive leadership-development experiences. His passion for the potential of these young people brought him to the attention of Scotland's Columba 1400 Community and International Leadership Centre on the Isle of Skye, where he served as the organization's first chief executive officer. He was named as the organization's first Fellow in 2004.

Chisholm is an avid skier, overlander and father of three. He lives with his partner in business and life, Anne-Marie Daniel, on Vancouver Island.

ROY GROUP

Working with you to develop your next generation of leaders.*

*by developing YOU as our next generation of mentors.

This book was designed as a gift.

Share it with those who have been a mentor to you and those who you sense are also on this path with you (or soon will be).

- For more information on bulk purchases and discounts, please contact **info@roygroup.net**.

- We would so appreciate it if you could be a messenger to your network about this book. Share a post of a key takeaway from this book on your social media and tag us at **@quietchampionsbook** and **#QuietChampions**.

- Leave a review on your online retailer of choice to connect the book with new readers.

- Visit **RoyGroup.net** for more information on why clients work with us and our approach of working with mentors to develop the next generation of leaders.

- Ask us to speak or convene a retreat for you and your team.

- Please reach out at **info@roygroup.net**.

www.ingramcontent.com/pod-product-compliance
Lightning Source LLC
Chambersburg PA
CBHW060351080526
44583CB00012B/260